Carrying
Grace to
Santiago

CARRYING GRACE TO SANTIAGO

A Daughter's Journey

MAUREEN LAURAN

With Illustrations by the Author

Buen Camino!

Maureen Lauran

April 1, 2013

WATERVIEW
PRESS

ALEXANDRIA VIRGINIA

CARRYING GRACE TO SANTIAGO
A Daughter's Journey
Copyright ©2011 by Maureen Lauran
ISBN-13-9781466451391
Printed in the United States of America

The poems of Rumi were taken from *The Essential Rumi*, translated
by Coleman Barks, with the generous permission of Coleman Barks.

You can order copies of *Carrying Grace to Santiago* through your local
bookstore or at Amazon.com.

For further information, contact:
Maureen Lauran
CarryingGracetoSantiago@gmail.com

For my brother, Frank,
just for being there.

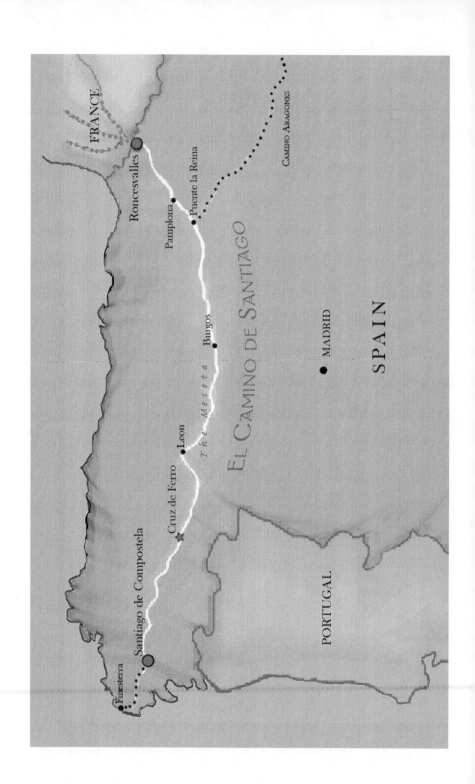

FRANCE

Roncesvalles

Pamplona

Puente la Reina

Camino Aragonés

Burgos

The Meseta

Leon

Cruz de Ferro

Santiago de Compostela

Finisterra

El Camino de Santiago

MADRID

SPAIN

PORTUGAL

Illustrations

ACKNOWLEDGMENTS

The walk I took to Santiago was a solitary one. The 500-miles I covered, carrying my mother's ashes for the greater part of them, provided me with limitless opportunities to make of the journey what I alone could make. Writing this book, however, the second journey I took with Grace, was not possible to make alone.

It was in Nick Reding's graduate class in creative writing at George Mason University, where the germ of this story began. Nick gave me thoughtfully written critiques which helped me look more carefully at the characters and where the "real story is."

I wish to express my gratitude to those who read the early drafts of my manuscript and willingly gave me both their time and their insightful comments: My high school friend, Beth Lippincott Scott, who read early drafts and shared some of her own family stories with me; Karen Dean Smith, who frequently visited Grace in her last years, offered balance and perspective in my concern for telling Grace's story with compassion; Karen Zens, who with her years and experiences in Spain, prepared me for some of the peculiarities of the Camino; my nieces, Emilie and Cynthia, who read looking for understanding. I hope they realized their goal.

I also want to mention Lisa Ferdenzi, Candida and Regina DeLuise, Phoebe Blake, and Colleen Garibaldi as well as Chawky Frenn, who read enough to encourage me to keep writing. David Hazard was among my most encouraging readers and graciously gave this project the benefit of his storytelling, and editorial skills. Thank you one and all.

Two colleagues at George Mason University were both generous with their time as well as their expertise: Lynne Constantine, who could uniquely speak to Grace's Italian immigrant experience, was an early reader who wrote concise critiques that nudged me to a clearer understanding of Grace's place on my pilgrimage. Also,

Helen Frederick, whose vast knowledge of printmaking and her ability to inspire exploration of the media was responsible for my looking for new ways of telling my story visually. I am privileged to have had them both on this "path" with me.

My debt to DeDe Casilli is beyond reckoning. In agreeing to read and edit my story, DeDe became editor, adviser, and friend. She spent many hours reading each installment I sent her and nearly an equal amount of time writing me her reactions, comments, and suggestions. She has been a fellow pilgrim in many ways.

It was only after finishing this writing that I returned to Elyn Aviva's very informative, *Following the Milky Way: A Pilgrimage on the Camino de Santiago*, and noticed we both quoted Cavafy's poem, "Ithaka." I quoted a part at the beginning of my story; she at the end of hers. For whatever subliminal influence her choice had on mine, I thank her.

My son, Michael, has been my greatest support throughout both of the journeys I took with Grace. From the time I first talked about walking the Camino, he showed his confidence in me and my ability to walk it and offered his unbridled encouragement. When I made the decision to go, he gave me gifts of a first aid kit, a water bottle and his obvious admiration. He remained always available to me as I began to weave Grace's story into my own. He offered his insights and asked meaningful questions about my intent. I am grateful that I was given the privilege of being his mother.

M.L.
Alexandria, VA
2011

CARRYING
GRACE TO
SANTIAGO

When you set out on your journey to Ithaca,
Pray that the road is long,
full of adventure, full of knowledge . . .
The Lestrygonians and the Cyclops,
the fierce Poseidon you will never encounter,
if you do not carry them within your soul,
if your heart does not set them up before you.

Constantine Cavafy

"Step out of line, ma'am, would you please?" ordered a young woman inspector as I passed through the metal detector archway. She let my large black tote bag roll on through the screening device after thoroughly scrutinizing the contents. The people in line behind me were becoming impatient. Some took their shoes and bags and shuffled to another line.

"Review over here, sir; when you're ready," she called out over her shoulder to a man in uniform. He exuded authority as he looked up from the neat piles of paperwork lying on the table in front of him. Surveying the next weighty situation he was being called to reconcile— my bag and me—he put his dark-rimmed glasses aside, and his mouth formed a tired smile.

"Just go on over there to that table, ma'am, and take that black box out of your bag for the inspector."

Something else cryptic passed between them but I didn't understand what it was. Several TSA inspectors reviewing other passengers' bags, turned to look my way and a couple of policemen stepped into view.

The inspector rose from his seat. "Good day, ma'am, an' how're yooo today? Good, good, well that's good." he said stiffly, after I told him I *had* been feeling fine.

"May I ask what you're carryin' in that black box, ma'am?" the officer drawled in a soft southern way as he gestured with his pencil toward the container that held Grace's ashes.

"Well, Officer, as I tried to explain to the young woman when I put my carry-on down, I have a box—it's sealed—with my mother's ashes in it. I wanted to take the box out of my bag before I put it through the X-ray machine but she insisted I just let it all ride through. I have a copy of her death certificate with me here, in the bag . . ."

"Now wait just a minute!" the officer said sharply, raising a cautionary hand as I reached toward my bag to retrieve the envelope that held the certificate. The two policemen walked over to the table to stand on either side of the inspector.

"Why don't you just step back a little and we'll take a closer look at this box, ma'am, if you would please. Let's have your passport too, ma'am." He looked very tense.

My ticket was tucked into my passport and I passed them both to him. My hands had started to shake and I was afraid he might have noticed.

After looking over my passport thoroughly, glancing up at me and back at the photo in it a couple of times, he turned the pages to see the visa stamps it carried. I pointed out the envelope in the black tote that had Grace's death certificate, he read that very carefully, too.

"So, now, let's see here—Where is it you're plannin' to take these ashes, ma'am?" He watched my eyes and my gestures carefully. Was he looking for nervousness or any inconsistency in the story I had already told him? (What is this? Time to practice on the passengers? Do I look like a criminal?)

"I'm taking them to Spain where I'm going to leave them." (Oh, geez, of course I'm going to leave them. What else? My mother loved air travel so much that I'm taking her ashes to Spain and back?) I was really beginning to worry that they weren't going to let me through inspection to board the plane. The airline people told me weeks ago that as long as I had the death certificate, there would be no problem.

The officer and one of the other TSA people had a whispered conference while other TSA inspectors standing nearby anxiously watched me. One of the whisperers in uniform produced a simple hand-held device with a removable piece of what looked like cloth on the end. He handed it to the inspector, who passed the cloth over all the edges and corners of the box. Somehow the piece of cloth determined that the contents were safe.

"All clear, ma'am. Thank you for your cooperation." His pleasure at being finished with me was obvious. "You have a good flight now, ya' hear?" He jotted something on my boarding pass, handed back my passport, ticket, death certificate, black box, and then gestured toward the boarding gate. He was as relieved as I was to have the ordeal over with.

Whew! I thought as I walked down the long aisle to find my flight's departure gate, Grace would simply not have been able to handle that kind of scrutiny. She got anxious just thinking about having to go out the front door. She would have left, or suggested I give up the whole idea and go home. I felt apologetic to her and smiled at myself. I was still watching out for her. Still feeling I had to protect her.

Several years before that flight I was about to take, I was flying home to Boston from a business trip and began thumbing through the in-flight travel magazine to pass the time. The issue was devoted to pilgrimage—from the narrowest meaning of the word to the broadest. There were a few inspiring stories by well-known writers—Alice Walker and John Berendt, among others—about their "quest" to a place that was pivotal for them in some deeply personal way.

Alice Walker wrote about her search for the burial place of Zora Neale Hurston, author, folklorist, and anthropologist, best known for her novel, *Their Eyes Were Watching God*. Walker learned that her literary inspiration had been buried in an unmarked grave and determined to find it. She wanted to give Hurston a memorial stone that was equal to the gift Walker felt she had been given through Hurston's writing.

John Berendt wrote about returning to Venice after many years of not seeing that magical city. He wrote about the pleasures of approaching Venice by crossing the lagoon in a boat from the airport rather than taking the more common route by bus and train that brought people into the bustling station at *Piazzale Roma*. The joy he took in watching Venice "arrive" slowly as it did for travelers for centuries before the Austrian land bridge was built, inspired me to do that very thing. I had been planning to revisit Venice with my son, after many years of not walking the quiet *calle* of *La Serenissima*. At Berendt's suggestion, when we got there, I hired a water taxi directly from Marco Polo Airport to the apartment where we would spend a couple of weeks.

Abigail Seymour's article about her walk on the Camino de Santiago, however, was especially inspiring to me. I had never heard of the 500-mile walk nor the 1,000-year old traditions which grew around it. Seymour described her own lessons in endurance and some of the highlights of her experiences on the path. She related the stories of many of the pilgrims she met and their reasons for making the pilgrimage. She told of the tradition of using the expression *"Ultreya!"* (Go beyond!) which pilgrims called out in greeting, encouraging each other to press on, keep going, reach further, as well as the frequently heard *"Buen Camino!"* (Good walk!) which serves to say many things like, "Have a good time!" "Enjoy yourself!" and "Safe journey!" One pilgrim told her, "You never get to Santiago, you only set out for it." Maybe that's true in all we do—we choose a road but the end isn't really the goal. All the events along the way alter the experience we expected and even the goal itself.

Just knowing about the Camino was thrilling. I never felt so excited about the possibility of having an adventure like that. I was consumed with the thought of it. Although it wasn't clear to me at the time when or how I'd someday find myself on the path to Santiago, I knew in some deep and unexplainable way that I too would walk the Way of St. James, as St. Francis himself had done and many other holy and not-so-holy pilgrims had for centuries before.

I began looking into the history of the Camino and reading what I could easily find about it. The actress Shirley MacLaine had written a popular book about her experiences on the Camino. There were other personal tales as well but I decided I wanted the cold hard facts—the history of it and how it got started, the tales and folk tales about it.

One book, written by an early walker, was full of historic information. Elyn Aviva's story, *Following the Milky Way*, was well researched if at times somewhat tedious. It also gave a thorough description of the difficulties in finding the path in those years when she walked before recent renewed interest in the pilgrimage had become so widespread. My best source of information, however, was the Confraternity of St. James, an organization set up by a few pilgrims who walked in the early 1980s and returned to England with a desire to help other pilgrims by giving them information, maps, and guides and a historic overview.

In the early Middle Ages hundreds of thousands of northern and central European pilgrims followed the ancient route to the tomb of Santiago, Saint James the Apostle. The tomb is in the crypt of the huge cathedral at Santiago de Compostela, in the western-most Spanish province of Galicia. Many walked for redemption in the belief that God would forgive all their sins and give them a new life after making the pilgrimage. Or that after suffering the trials of the long walk to Santiago, He would heal them of disease. The route is lined with crumbling and some surviving Romanesque monasteries, churches, and chapels, hospitals, hospices, and hostels that grew up along the path to serve the pilgrims. Santiago de Compostela was considered one of the three most important places of pilgrimage in the Christian faith, the other two being Jerusalem and Rome.

The apostle James was sent to preach in Spain, and according to church history, he returned to Palestine after several years of missionary work. In 44 A.D., shortly after his return, Herod Agrippa beheaded him. The legend tells of St. James' followers putting his body on a ship that returned to Galicia, guided by angels. He was buried in a tomb and his burial place was lost for centuries until a hermit (guided by a star) discovered it around the year 813. Alphonso II had a church begun on the site sometime thereafter. The event of the discovery of the saint's bones was what was to have initiated the pilgrimage, but historically, the beginning of the pilgrimage is dated to around 880 or 890 A.D. In fact, going back still further, there's evidence of early man and the Romans having used the pathway west as well.

During the height of the popularity of the walk, from 1000 AD to around 1200 AD, hundreds of thousands of pilgrims made their way to visit St. James' shrine. The Turks were blocking their way to Jerusalem, so Santiago de Compostela and Rome became the two primary destinations of the religious as well as "seekers" of many other stripes. The hordes of pilgrims, charlatans, thieves and saints who passed through the area of northern Spain brought the development of many villages, towns and cities that have become some of the most important economic and cultural centers of present day Spain. Cities like Pamplona, Burgos, León, all owe much of their social and economic growth to the immense impact the pilgrims made on the area as they traveled to and from Santiago.

In its earliest manifestations, the route was a network of various paths that didn't resemble the route taken today in the least. There were paths running east and west throughout Europe, which formed an interconnection of trails and roadways, all meeting the main route at

Puente la Reina, in the province of Navarra, well within the border of Spain. From that point, the Camino continues west for another approximately 450 miles. It ambles through the cities of Estella, Logroño, Santo Domingo de la Calzada, Burgos, León, Astorga, Ponferrada and finally into the province of Galicia and on to the city of Santiago de Compostela itself. That main part of the pilgrimage is known as the *Via Franca, Camino Francés*, or the "French Way." Its name comes from the numbers of French pilgrims who walked it, or some say it got its name quite simply because it was the route *from* France—as distinguished from the routes from the south of Spain or from Portugal.

In Santiago the huge and ornate cathedral, in the Spanish Gothic style, with spires and bells and carvings of saints and sinners and angels is where the reliquary with the saintly bones are kept, supposedly in the very spot where they were found. Pilgrims made their way there, walking, riding a horse, in a cart or now, by bicycle, bus, train or in the family car. Today people who aren't able to take the time out of their busy lives to walk the entire Camino will walk the path in segments over a period of years—two weeks to cover one stretch, then two weeks to cover another section another year, until they've finally arrived in Santiago.

To allow for more easy tourism to Santiago, the provincial Galician overseers of the rules of the pilgrimage not long ago determined that a pilgrim could receive all the benefits of the completed pilgrimage by walking a minimum of 100-kilometers or, approximately 62 miles. The 100-kilometer waymarker is well within the boundaries of the province of Galicia, where the city of Santiago is. This special allowance has gone a long way toward improving tourism in Galicia and in helping the impoverished province with its economic recovery.

Early pilgrims usually traveled in groups for safety from highwaymen as well as any number of other misfortunes they might encounter— including sickness, accident and famine. There have been many literary references to the life of the pilgrims from early writers both well known and unknown. Chaucer and Shakespeare have made reference to the Camino and contemporary writers still find pilgrimage rich fodder for metaphor and allegory. In the last years of her life, Edith Wharton made the pilgrimage to Santiago two times. Her chauffeur drove her.

The typical medieval pilgrim wore a cloak and a wide-brimmed hat with a scallop shell attached to it to identify himself as a pilgrim and to replicate the often seen image of St. James himself. The shell is

one of the attributes of St. James because of an early association to a legend of his rising out of the sea to battle the Moors. It's become the symbol of the Camino de Santiago pilgrimage itself. Not unlike present day pilgrims who sometimes still wear a scallop shell around their neck or pinned to their backpack, those early pilgrims walked with a long staff, replaced today by collapsible high-tech walking sticks; a leather bag for their personal things which purpose is fulfilled today by a lightweight backpack; and a water flask, now replaced with various kinds of plastic containers or high-tech, temperature efficient, lightweight thermos bottles. Whatever the changes in gear, however, the majority of pilgrims continue to walk for the same reasons: redemption, adventure, health, friendship, recreation, enlightenment or for just the sport of it.

The original hostels that were built along the path were mainly run by Benedictine and Cluniac monks and today many are still run by various orders of the Catholic Church. Other rest stops, hostels and *refugios* have been set-up by community organizations that see the advantages of attracting the pilgrims to their businesses. And, as was true a thousand years ago, some others are privately owned by entrepreneurs ready to cash in on the needs for food and shelter of the thousands of walkers making their way to Santiago.

A few years after reading that Abigail Seymour magazine article about the Camino, I was sitting in a restaurant in Washington, D.C. with two friends who knew I was interested in the walk. I was confronted with the inevitable question:

"So, Maureen, when do you think you're going to go?" said Colleen whose birthday we were celebrating.

No one had actually put it to me so directly. As though it was a fact that I would go, and only the date was needed to confirm it as a reality.

"Well, I don't know," I took a sip of my wine. "Maybe this summer. Yeah, sure—if I go right after classes are over. Maybe I can take the time before starting a job I've got lined up to carry me through the summer."

7

I responded without thinking. I was teaching at a university outside of the city and doing some freelance design work as well. Having the summers open made it possible for me to take the five weeks I thought I'd need to complete the walk. Many people finish it in four weeks, sometimes just under that, but I thought it unlikely that I'd be able to walk twenty miles a day, every day, and decided five weeks would be more realistic for me.

The decision to take my mother's ashes with me came almost as an afterthought. From time-to-time I had asked my brother what he thought we should do with the ashes I had been holding onto for about a year. My father had died nearly forty years before Grace. He was buried in a family plot in Troy, New York, where ashes weren't accepted—even if there had been room for her. I asked my son and my uncle, her brother. I asked my friends for ideas, or inspiration. What I got were some very odd suggestions from my very creative friends, like hiring a plane or helicopter and "drizzling" her out the window over a favorite place of hers (she didn't have any "favorite place"), or putting her ashes in a paper bag, punching some holes in the bag and walking around New York City where she grew up. In the end, everyone I asked only encouraged me to do whatever I felt comfortable with.

I did want to find a place to put Grace's ashes that would in some way be "exceptional" and that would place her in a larger context than she had experienced in her life. I liked the idea of carrying "Grace," with me on my walk. It could also be a symbolic way of leaving the memories of her and the weight of the responsibility I had always felt for her at some significant place and walking on. Being done with it. Surely such a heroic gesture would put her presence in my life at rest, would it not?

***

"Did you remember the bread?" she barked at me as I entered her dimly lit room.

"Yup, I've got it."

It was a Sunday afternoon in late fall. The skies were clear blue and the air was chilly. I was making my weekly visit to Grace at the nursing home where she had been living for the past five years. And, I had my plastic bag of stale bread.

"Well, here, take mine." She leaned over from the chair where she was sitting next to the only window in the room and opened the door in her bedside table. Every breakfast, lunch, and dinner tray that arrived in her room came with at least two slices of thin white bread that she ferreted away for our Sunday afternoons with the sea gulls.

"Okay, I'll go get the wheelchair. Here, you put on your coat." I stood behind her and held out her coat. "It's cold out today. Better wear your hat. I brought you a new pair of gloves; yours were looking pretty ratty." I had become the one in charge. She was no longer the raging tyrant, the neglectful, abusive mother but just an old woman for whom I had compassion. Our caretaker roles had reversed many years before.

Grace was nearly ninety years old and, thankfully, still clear headed. She was also still furious with the world. But her anger could no longer hurt me. I had learned that there was no telling what she might be angry about on any given day. Was I late today? Yes, a little, as usual. Me, who prided myself on being prompt, somehow I always managed to show up late for our Sunday afternoon outings.

Out on the street, I felt the fresh air on my face and drew in a deep breath. "Ah, breathe, Mom. It's good to get the air in your lungs. Keeps your head clear too." I doubt that she ever really did take a big breath, just to be obstinate, but I knew being out of the stale-smelling nursing home was good for both of us.

Pushing her wheelchair down the sidewalk the few blocks to the park on Boston Harbor, I could already sense the gathering of the birds.

"Hey, Ma, I think they know you're coming! Look at all of them circling and flying over to our spot!"

"Oh, they don't recognize me. Don't be silly."

"Well, they might just know us because of the wheelchair and because they've figured out that we're always here on Sundays." I offered.

Whether the birds anticipated her arrival or not, Grace so completely enjoyed the adventure of going to feed them the bread she saved that I never wanted her to miss this one weekly event. Even in rain, we'd make the walk. Even when it snowed. Even when I teased her in the middle of winter when only a few gulls swooped down around her chair. "Well, who knows, maybe they're wintering on the Cape."

Her face softened as she saw the shadows of them surrounding her through her nearly blind eyes. Sometimes she felt she hadn't saved enough bread which is why she asked me to bring extra. Whether we had a lot or a little, the whole feeding was over in a very few minutes. She seemed genuinely, if fleetingly, happy.

At the airport in Madrid, I claimed my backpack from the carousel, put Grace inside it, along with a few toiletries, the flip-flops I wore on the flight over and a book I was reading—I can't remember what—nothing about the Camino, I'm sure. I pulled-on my hiking boots and stuffed my carry-on bag away in the pack along with some photocopied pages about the Camino from a Lonely Planet guide, *Walking in Spain*, that a friend had given me. Though I had hiked with my new backpack loaded down on my daily and weekly practice walks, I wasn't prepared for the heft of it after the flight. Hoisting the backpack on for the first time was a surprise and I staggered with the weight of it. As I struggled to gain my balance, I thought, *I'll have to do better than this. Allez-Oop! Here we go, Grace!*

Chamartin Train Station, an ultra-modern facility in the northern district of Madrid, is part of the metro system and easily reached from the airport. From Chamartin I would take a late afternoon express train to Pamplona, in the province of Navarra and not far from the French border. From there my plans were to reach the monastery in the mountains at Roncesvalles by bus the next day. If all went according to schedule, I'd begin my walk from Roncesvalles on the day after that.

The train eased slowly out of the station and through the congested out-lying towns surrounding Madrid. It sped northward, past ancient villages, towns and cities—Guadalajara, Catalayud, Paracuellos, Morata de Jalon, Tello di Novara. Old villages and crumbling fortified castles on hilltops looked deserted now though they were probably thriving centers when the early pilgrims were setting out for Santiago. I dug into my backpack to find the small box of nutrition bars a friend had sent me for my trip and devoured four of them. They were my only meal that day. I breathed a deep sigh of satisfaction and settled back to enjoy the scenes of Spain hurtling past my window.

The crisply uniformed conductor walked through the car where I was sitting, calling out "Pamplona! (something . . . something) Pamplona!" The trip had gone by quickly. I was glad I heard him announce our arrival because I had gotten mixed-up with counting the cities we passed before reaching Pamplona and it was getting too dark to see any station signs through the windows. I got my backpack on well before the train slowed outside the station and headed toward the exit door. The train swayed and bumped along before coming to a slow and lurching stop. Others stood and joined me in the line, ready to descend.

As I make my slow pilgrimage through
the world,
a certain sense of beautiful mystery seems
to gather and grow.

Arthur Christopher Benson

It was very dark when I walked through the deserted station and out onto the street. There were no hotels nearby as I had expected, so I followed a few people walking briskly ahead of me up the hill toward the walled city center. With every step I was falling further and further behind them. It was a long incline on a sidewalk that followed a dimly lit street. I was approaching two young men sitting on a bench, sharing a bottle and having a heated debate or at least, they were yelling at each other about something. They saw me coming and when I was right in front of them, both jumped up in unison, made an aggressive jab at me, yelled something and then fell back in laughter. Even though I would have had to struggle with the fact that I knew practically no Spanish and my Spanish phrase book was at the bottom of my backpack, my choice to not take a taxi from the station seemed pretty stupid.

Breathless and panting, I followed the sidewalk through the large portal in the ancient walls and into the relative safety of the historic center. There was no one else on the well-lighted streets. Directly in front of me was a sign that showed a symbol of a bed with an arrow pointing left. It was past eleven o'clock—five in the morning for me—and I had been traveling for almost twenty-four hours. The first hotel I came to would be just perfect, regardless of how it looked. As it happened, it looked really swanky and had a few stars trailing its name. Surely real pilgrims wouldn't take such lodgings, but I forgave myself the indulgence as I strode inside and up to the registration desk.

"Good evening, madam," the uniformed woman behind the desk said in perfect English. "May I help you?"

Did I detect a note of disdain? Surely my backpack and rumpled clothes weren't that unusual to see in a hotel with stars.

"Yes, please, I'm hoping you have a single room available," I replied, noticing that she knew I wasn't Spanish and wondering what else she might have thought I would be inquiring about at that hour. My fatigue was not helping my mood.

After I unbuckled my backpack and worked my arms out of the straps, I reached for my passport and credit card in the money pouch tucked under my shirt. I signed the register, she wrote down my passport number and then checked on vacant rooms. She handed me a plastic card key and pointed to the small elevator across from the registration desk.

"*Gracias, muchas gracias,*" I tried out my few Spanish words. "*Buenos noches,*" I added. She softened just a bit and smiled in return.

"Have a good rest, madam."

A few minutes later I was in a room, beautifully decorated with soft rose-colored walls and what looked like reproduction 18th century French furniture with paintings of Spanish landscapes and bullfights on the walls. The bathroom was by contrast, very contemporary with stylish sink and tub and wonderful smelling soaps, lotions, crémes, and shampoo. *Ah-h-h-h.*

After a delicious hot shower, I crawled between the crisp sheets that smelled of lavender and dropped off into a sound sleep. As I drifted off I remember thinking, *I made it. It's really happening! I'm here. I'll be walking on the Camino de Santiago—soon!*

The next day I woke at noon and dressed quickly, re-packed my bag and carried it down to the lobby to look for a place to get a cup of coffee. At a bar next to the hotel I settled into a booth and ordered two croissant-like pastries and two cups of rich, frothy coffee. I was completely satisfied and excited to begin the next part of my adventure.

Anxious about not missing the bus to Roncesvalles later in the day, I walked to the Tourist Information Office, got a map of Pamplona, and headed for the bus station first, to be sure I knew where it was. Secure in its location and how to get there, I spent a couple of hours looking around that area of Pamplona and trying to get accustomed to the full weight of my backpack.

Before leaving home, I had pared down what I would take with me to what I considered very essential. Adding Grace's ashes, though, pushed the weight I'd have to carry to more than thirty pounds—well over the fifteen to twenty pounds that was recommended by everyone who knew anything about long-distance hiking. I silently determined I'd simply have to get stronger.

Back at the bus station later that afternoon, I had my first encounter with a fellow pilgrim. He was a round and bearded Irish priest. He fell into conversation easily with anyone interested in talking. He had spent several years as a missionary in Chile and, even through his soft Irish brogue, it was obvious he spoke fluent Spanish listening to him chat with the others. We were standing with a group of about ten people who had gathered to wait for the once-daily, six o'clock bus that took the road into the Pyrenees Mountains to Roncesvalles. The Priest told me he was living in Melbourne, Australia and editing a journal that was published by the church. He was taking some time off to "rest and reflect." As we waited, the group mingled with one another and shared their reasons and motivations for walking the Camino.

"I'm gonna walk ta thank God fa ma beautiful life," The Priest said.

I was surprised to realize that gratitude might be a possible motivation for a priest to take such a challenging walk—he wasn't asking for anything. He wasn't expecting any certain outcome. He had no agenda. He was just walking and being thankful. I was humbled. Unlike him, I had a lot of reasons for walking and wanted to get a lot out of the walk and I had a lot of expectations. His words were to become a refrain that haunted me at times when I would lose confidence that I would make it—when I thought I couldn't go on.

"Gratitude fa bein' har a'tall is what I'm feelin' right nue. You jus' can't imagine how many thin's had ta fall inta place for me ta be standin' har!" The Priest added. But, indeed, I think many of us could imagine. Heads nodded and people chuckled in agreement. It seemed everyone held a sense of disbelief that they were actually there.

CARRYING GRACE TO SANTIAGO

The Irish Priest wasn't dressed in clothes I expected a priest to be wearing. He had on brown cotton pants and a striped short-sleeved shirt, open at the collar. He was carrying very little with him, considering the five hundred miles ahead of us. Most of the rest of those waiting had full-fledged backpacks; The Priest, only a small, lightweight day pack. He was tall and very robust, overweight really, fully into middle age with no signs of having been particularly active in the years before. His florid complexion suggested more than just his happy nature—maybe high blood pressure? Helping to load the packs and gear of the other pilgrims onto the bus made him breathless. He wiped his brow with a rumpled cotton handkerchief that he drew from his pants pocket after hoisting the bags into place. I shook my head and silently wondered how he'd ever make it to Santiago.

Our driver had been standing in a glass-enclosed bus company office with two or three other men—smoking cigarettes, talking and laughing. Finally he stepped out of the cloud of smoke, tossed his cigarette on the ground, and walked to our idling bus. After pushing a button to open the door, he swung into his seat. With a toot of his horn, he signaled our imminent departure. We all formed a haphazard line and filed onto the bus to take a seat. I wanted a window.

The bus was large, and relatively new with enormous windows that gave each rider (window or aisle) a clear view of what there was to see. The driver backed the behemoth out of its stall and onto the busy, rush hour streets. We drove east out of the city and up the valley of the River Arga. Urban sprawl cloaked the distinction between the in-lying smaller villages and the city itself. It was difficult to see these clusters of houses as anything more than suburbs. Many people who had gotten on with the pilgrims at the bus station or as the bus ambled through the serpentine city streets, began to reach their destinations as we passed through these centers.

Finally we started to climb. Occasionally the driver tooted the horn in greeting to someone walking along the roadside. We stopped in several small villages—two or three houses, a market, a bar, an old chapel—where one or two people got off the bus. Families were standing nearby, watching for the bus's arrival and children ran out to meet it—their only connection to the world beyond, it seemed.

We passed through Zubiri ("village of the bridge"—there were so many villages with bridges!) and on to the Puerto de Erro where my ears started to feel the pressure of the altitude we were reaching. Continuing up the valley we reached Burquete which is famous for its white houses with red shutters, called *caserios* (farmhouses) typical of this Basque countryside. Hemingway chose Burquete as the trout-fishing setting in *The Sun Also Rises*, so it also carries that distinction for literary tourists. Villagers waved in response to the driver's toots and, sometimes, just to say *"Hola!"* It seemed a familiar part of their day and I waved back wanting to be a part of it.

The driver brought the bus through hairpin turns—up and up. We were climbing for over an hour past high, steep green pastures with brown cows grazing languorously. The hills were so steep that the cows seemed to be hanging there in some illusory way. Many long-haired sheep wandered slowly through still other pastures. They were square looking with their shaggy, black and brown manes hanging to the ground covering the evidence of their legs. No doubt magic there again, or was it velcro?

The hospice and monastery built at Roncesvalles to care for the pilgrims became among the most famous and important of its kind on the entire Camino. The large Augustinian abbey was founded in 1130 and still serves as a monastery to a small community of monks overseeing the registration of the pilgrims. They're given the responsibility of maintaining the historical and religious traditions of the pilgrimage as well. Keeping records of the numbers of people walking, why they walk, and when, is a large part of their duties.

There are now two privately owned restaurants, and a hotel near the abbey, the ruin of an old chapel, and a small church used mostly by the pilgrims as well as a scattering of other buildings that make up the enclave. Those who began their walk in France, England, Germany and beyond reach Roncesvalles through the mountain pass from Saint-Jean Pied de Port on the French side of the border and sometimes rest at Roncesvalles in the large *refugio* for a day before continuing. As the bus pulled up, people were sitting on benches and the grass, talking to one another or reading and resting in the remaining early evening light. There was laundry drying on a nearby fence—socks and shirts waving greetings to the new arrivals.

"Hola, señora, señor. Welcome!" the woman behind the desk called out as the Irish Priest and I entered the office where we were to register with the rest of our group.

"No, no, we're not together," I rushed to say. The Priest explained to the woman in Spanish and she apologized incessantly for some respectable amount of time in keeping with the error. Fearing she might have offended The Priest by assuming he had a personal relationship with me, she took especially good care of us in the registration process. Her solicitous demeanor became irritating and I was surprised again at my annoyance. If I couldn't find some tolerance for her, I feared my own absolution was doubtful.

As others who had arrived on the bus with us gathered around the table where we were to complete the registration, the woman passed out copies of a form. We filled-in our name, address, country of origin and official country passport number and then there were a few other questions to determine whether one was walking for religious or spiritual reasons or if the walk was for recreation. The monks keep records of the numbers of people walking, their country of origin, and their purpose for making the pilgrimage. There's no reason given as to why they want that information and no suggestion as to how long they've been collecting it but I assumed the numbers must have historic or logistical significance.

After registering and paying a small fee, I was handed my Pilgrim's Passport, a multi-folded sheet identifying me as a registered pilgrim who was entitled to all the privileges of that position. The starting date is recorded there and the passport receives its first of many ornate and colorful stamps. Most importantly, the Pilgrim's Passport, when you get it stamped regularly at each *refugio* or hostel where you sleep, allows you to have a bed in the next hostel the following night. Essential for taking advantage of the minimal cost for a bed in the *refugio*s along the way, most pilgrims guard their Pilgrim's Passport as they do their cash.

There were signs around the compound directing pilgrims to the chapel for the evening Pilgrim's Blessing, a 12th century tradition which takes place daily. The chapel was a short walk from where we had registered. I checked my watch, and realized the appointed hour was soon but I wanted to claim a bed for the night before walking over to the service.

The large stone building that had been converted into a dormitory-like refuge for pilgrims was, in fact, the first building I had seen when the bus arrived in Roncesvalles. The interior had been recently renovated and modernized with large bathroom facilities downstairs and one large open room just a few steps above ground level. There was a sea of bunkbeds that stretched the full length and width of the building's main floor. I wandered through the rows of beds looking for one that didn't seem already claimed with a backpack, clothes, or a walking stick resting on it. At last there was one with no obvious tenant and I rested my backpack against it. I spread-out my sleeping bag on the uncovered mattress, as I saw that others had done, and slid the backpack under the bed. With a brief look back to make a note of which row my bunk was in, I made a stop in the downstairs toilet and raced out of the building to follow groups of people who were hurrying toward the chapel for the service.

The 12th century Romanesque chapel, *Sancti Spiritus*, held several dozen of us. I was sitting at the end of a pew at the left side and halfway back from the altar. There were beautiful stained glass windows on all sides of the room and some narrow, especially tall ones in the apse behind the altar. As the service began with the sound of one of the monks singing, the atmosphere was hushed. Light came from a few candles glowing on the altar and the gleam of a gilded crucifix and other glistening things set out on the table at the altar—candlesticks, a chalice and a tray—which were the focus of some lights mounted high on the massive columns that defined the nave. My eyes filled with tears as I recognized the significance of being about to take part in this ancient tradition. The feeling of fulfillment was overwhelming—and I hadn't even started walking yet.

Looking out at those who had gathered. Some heads were bowed reverently, some looking about the chapel at the stained-glass windows, some were looking down, reading—in a prayer book, or perhaps a guidebook. Others, like myself, gazed around with awe at the quiet scene taking place once again in this small chapel in the mountains as it had for a thousand years before.

Sitting listening to the five monks singing, I thought of one of the last conversations I had with Grace about plans for her funeral.

"Well, whatever you do, don't give me a Catholic service! I don't want anything to do with that church!" Grace demanded.

It was one of several talks I tried to have with her about what she wanted me to do when she died.

"I dunno," she said with a wave of her hand as if brushing off the whole topic. "Just throw me away. Put me in a Pauper's Grave. I don't want you to be wasting any money on me," she muttered with her head bowed and venom in her voice.

Oh, brother, she really wouldn't like what's going on here.

As the priest leading the service spoke first in Spanish, then in French, German, and English, the group's attention was clearly on the words of the ancient prayer: The Confraternity of St. James publishes a translation of a pilgrim's blessing that was used on the Camino since the 1200s.

> Oh God, be a companion for them along the path,
> a guide at crossroads, strength in their weariness,
> defense before dangers, shelter on the way, shade
> against heat, light in the darkness, a comforter in
> their discouragements, and firmness in their
> intentions, in order that, through your guidance,
> they might arrive unscathed at the end of their
> journey and, enriched with graces and virtues,
> they might return safely to their homes, which
> now lament their absence, filled with salutary and
> lasting joy.

Response　　　Amen

> May the Lord direct your steps with his approval,
> and be your inseparable companion on the entire
> camino.

Response　　　Amen

> May the Virgin Mary grant you her maternal pro-
> tection, defend you in all dangers of soul and
> body, and may you merit to arrive safely at the
> end of your pilgrimage under her mantle.

Response　　　Amen

> May the Archangel Rafael accompany you on the
> Camino as he accompanied Tobias, and protect
> you from every injury and obstacle.

Response　　　Amen

Next to where I sat was a beautiful stained-glass window with figures, symbols, plants and patterns in it. Looking more closely at the main figure, I realized it was the image of the Archangel Michael (my son's name is Michael). A good omen.

After the service, I joined some other people who decided to take advantage of the dinner available for a small fee. It was being served in the dining hall of still another building near the chapel. We were told the choice was either fresh local trout or pasta, each with its own side dish of a different vegetable.

I entered the large room with a group of diners. We found several round tables with white cotton tablecloths arranged around a cream colored room. Saints watched from every wall and two or three crucifixes hovered above our heads. I pulled out a chair at a table and joined a group of seven or eight other new arrivals.

Across the table there were two middle-aged Italian brothers from Pordenone, not far from Venice and near Grado where I had spent a year studying art and traveling around Italy. I was happy to be able to carry on a simple conversation with them. They were pleased that I knew their hometown. They were both retired and wanted to have an adventure together before they got too old and couldn't make such a demanding walk.

On my left was a young Australian woman who assisted a celebrity chef in Sydney. She wanted to escape the kitchen and get some exercise. Her plan was to walk as fast as she could and finish the entire walk in less than three weeks. After our dinners were served, she tasted her choice of pasta and, with dramatic affect, abruptly pushed her plate away. I enjoyed the trout and relished the delicious fresh vegetables that were evidently grown by the resident monks. A basket of still-warm breads were passed around the table. There was a large pitcher of red wine that circled the table, too. The chef's assistant decided not to try the wine. More for the rest of us.

On my right was an elderly couple from France and the woman's sister. They were very lighthearted and seemed happy about everything—bubbling over whenever another course was served at the table or at some remark made by a fellow diner. They spoke a little English and I was able to understand that they liked to hike together and planned a budget holiday walking a part of the Camino and paying the nominal fees at the pilgrims' *refugios*. They had no thought of finishing the entire walk. They had planned a two-week holiday and would take a train home to a town near Toulouse from wherever they found themselves at the end of the two weeks.

The Irish Priest was also at my table. He chose the fish for his dinner and was delighted to finish the Australian Chef's plate of pasta and the extra bread brought to our table at his request. He spoke to those of us who understood English with what began to sound like sub-titles as he switched to Italian to include the brothers from Pordenone and to French to include the *Ménage á Trois*. The Catholic newsletter he had been editing for several years was published in Spanish for the brotherhood of missionaries who worked in developing countries in Central and South America, so of course, as he proved earlier at the bus station in Pamplona, he would have been able to offer sub-titles in Spanish had there been the need.

The Priest said he didn't plan to walk the entire Camino but intended to take the train or, sometimes go by bus if he wasn't up to walking or the weather was bad. Following such a flexible plan, he saw no reason that he wouldn't fulfill his life-long dream of reaching Santiago. All heads nodded in agreement. I breathed a sigh of relief.

People leaving the dining room filed out chatting; some gathered in groups outside the doorway. Several people stood shivering waiting for friends to join them, zipping up their jackets and pulling on sweaters against the cold mountain air. A group of five or six British men were heading to the restaurant nearby and called out an invitation to anyone interested in joining them for a drink. It was almost ten o'clock so I decided to forego the gathering at the bar.

Stuffing my hands in the pockets of my windbreaker, I walked hurriedly back to the dormitory to get ready for bed. Counting across and down the rows of bunkbeds, I found mine easily. As it happened, The Irish Priest and The Australian Chef shared a bunk across from me. The Priest was on top and The Chef below. He struggled up to his nest and drew a thin cloth over himself, said "Good night" to anyone listening, and made a wish for the lights to go out. As if on cue, the lights did go out and the room started to quiet down.

Several people walked through the aisles with a toothbrush in hand, a kit with personal things, and a towel thrown over an arm or shoulder. I gathered up my toothbrush, paste, soap container and the piece of lightweight cotton fabric I planned to use as a towel and a wrap-up after showering. The women's bathroom was very busy and word went out that there was no more hot water. The luxurious shower I had taken the night before would have to do. I brushed my teeth, gave my face a quick swipe with cold water and headed back to my bunk.

Lying in bed, it took me quite awhile to settle down. The earplugs I was sure I'd brought weren't to be found. I dug in my backpack for them briefly and then just decided to do without them that first night. I was aware of all the people around me—top, front, back, and in every direction. Some people made very peculiar sounds as they slept. Others murmured in quiet conversation. The Chef kept making a *"tsk"*ing sound every time The Priest moved. Evidently his shifting around upstairs caused a surge at her level. At some point I finally dropped off and slept deeply.

When I woke in the morning, everyone around me was gone. I wondered what time it was and, checking my watch, saw it was only seven-thirty. There were still some other stragglers standing near their bunks but the vast majority of pilgrims were on their way. I thought maybe I had missed something—a signal that was intended to be the "START." I grabbed my toothbrush, hurried downstairs to the toilets, back up to my bunk to stuff my sleeping bag into my backpack and pull on my boots. I zipped on my windbreaker and hoisted the pack up and hooked an arm into a strap, turned and grabbed the other. Buckling it at my waist, I rushed to the door.

The morning sun hadn't yet come over the mountain when I walked out. There was a soft mist that had settled on the enclave. I looked around to orient myself and saw only brief glimpses of stone and the road that softly dissolved again into a hazy vision. The sign that stood pointing to the Camino came into sight and I turned and walked in that direction. The quiet stillness of the morning was interrupted by the crunch of my boots on the pebbled earth and the sound of cowbells nearby, trumpeting my first steps on the path. As I passed an ancient stone cross that marks the Camino at the edge of Roncesvalles, I realized there were tears streaming down my cheeks.

I travel for travel's sake. The great affair is to
move: to feel the needs and hitches of our life
more nearly; to come down of this feather-bed
of civilization, and find the globe granite under-
foot and strewn with cutting flints . . .And
when the present is so exacting, who can annoy
himself about the future?

Robert Louis Stevenson

"I t's difficult to find the markers even when you know what you're looking for, but I'm sure it's this way!" the woman said, pointing to the left, in the obvious direction of the path.

The older couple was in Pamplona the day before when I first walked down the mountains from Roncesvalles. He looked weathered, as though he spent a lot of time outdoors. She was flushed and seemed to be still in the throes of getting accustomed to hiking in the brutal, record-breaking heat of northern Spain. With guidebooks in hand and fully outfitted with backpacks, high-tech, lightweight walking sticks, and sturdy walking shoes, they were debating then about which way to go to the pilgrim's *refugio* in the center of town. Today it was also which way to turn.

"No, see the way the rocks are laid out?" he replied. "They're arranged in a cairn but the top one is turned to the right, not the left."

"Yes, dear," she said with obvious strain, "but those people who passed ahead of us walked to the left, and the path is clearly worn that way." she raised her arm and pointed purposefully toward the walkers in the distance. "Here comes someone, let's see which way she walks."

"Hola," I said as I approached the couple. Hoping that maybe they wouldn't know that I spoke English and understood what they were saying, I raised my hand to wave and kept walking. Maybe I could avoid refereeing this dance of theirs.

"Aren't you that American woman who's carrying her mother's ashes?" the woman asked.

Caught.

"Yes, I am," I said, then thought, *and you're the 'Bickering Brits' I've been avoiding.* Anyone making the walk learns quickly who else is on the path a few days ahead or behind him or her. People stop to rest and chat along the way or talk about other pilgrims they've met when they reach a *refugio.* I wasn't surprised that the Bickering Brits knew who I was, just taken back by the way they described me.

"Tell me, dear, if you don't mind, isn't the stone on the top of this cairn suggesting that the path turns here and goes to the left?" asked the man raising his arm and punching his walking stick into the air.

Since I didn't speak Spanish, or French, and there was no hope of my understanding what the Germans were saying, I'd had long hours of no conversation at all. My walk had been that much more solitary. I liked it that way. People who walked with a friend or in a group just seemed to be walking and talking, walking and talking. I wondered if they noticed the lush color of the mountains, the fields of soft pink, purple, and yellow flowers, the different rhythms of the songbirds and insects. But then, who was I to say how everyone else should walk their walk? In fact, I began to realize that in all of my preparations, I hadn't given much thought to the other people who would be walking.

I realized it was something I didn't have any control over and I could either keep feeling annoyed by this one or that one or relax a little about people's idiosyncrasies. I had only walked a total of about fifty miles and had been getting irritated by people more than I ordinarily do, and certainly more than I wanted to. *You don't get to choose who's going to show up on your path, Maureen.* I counseled myself. Or do you? As the miles passed, I began to recognize that the people I met were often there at my bidding—for good or ill—a mirror of what I myself was feeling or thinking about at the time.

Two women, one American and one Belgian, were walking behind me as I left a cafe in the mountains outside Burquete the day before meeting up with the Brits. I heard them talking rapidly for at least five minutes before they rounded a bend and came into sight. Voices carry so much further in the hills and valleys where there are few other sounds.

I paused under a tree to take my pack off and get at my water bottle; hoping they'd pass me so I could avoid the *rat-a-tat-tat* of their talk and return to the quiet of my own thoughts.

"Hey! How ya' doin'? Tired, huh? Isn't this great? I think I'll lose a few pounds before the week's out! How far ya' goin' today? We're gonna stay in that nice *refugio* at Larrasoaña tonight. Wanna' join us?" rattled the American.

"No thanks. I'll take a rest here and maybe have something to eat. Not sure how far I'll go today. I might see you there. Enjoy your walk. *Bon Camino!*"

And so now here were the Bickering Brits.

"Actually, I didn't know that the top rock was supposed to indicate direction," I answered. "I think I'm going to the right, though, no matter what that rock's saying. Besides, there're some other pilgrims up ahead. You can just make them out." I pointed to the same group of people his partner had pointed to. The group was beginning their ascent up the mountain, mere specs beyond the field of tall golden grasses.

It seemed absurd to suggest the path was going in another direction than the one worn down and obviously followed for centuries. I wondered what the real issue was. Could this whole walk be an opportunity for them to adjust to life in retirement together? Maybe they hoped to form some new lines of communication by sharing this experience and learning more about each other. They weren't off to a very good start.

I set my pack down, resting it against my leg, and straightened up to take off my wide-brimmed straw hat and wipe my brow with my sleeve. Even though spring in Spain, and all of Europe in fact, were having some of the hottest days on record, I was wearing my one long-sleeved shirt. The sun burned my skin even through the shirt. I was grateful for a rest from the weight of my backpack and a chance to take a drink.

"Yes, quite so. Thank you very much." The man seemed deflated and walked off briskly, placing his long wooden walking stick firmly in the dusty earth. His wife scurried quickly after him. "Thanks, dear, *bon Camino! Ultreya!*" she called out weakly.

"*Bon Camino,*" I called in return.

When is it that we begin to shift to the Spanish "*buen?*" Maybe when we've gone further from the French border? Or, maybe since this part of the Camino is called "the French way," we continue with "*bon*" all the way to Santiago? Or, were people saying "*buen*" and I just couldn't tell the difference? As with so much on the walk, I'd learn as I went along.

I sat on a clump of earth at the edge of the path and took a long drink of water. Once again, I wanted to let the Brits walk on to create more distance between us.

Except for the afternoon heat, the weather had been perfect until then—clear blue skies, high fluffy clouds. Now that I was out of the Pyrenees, the mornings were no longer so cold and I could walk comfortably without putting on every piece of clothing in my pack. In fact, I had brought very little to wear. I used my rain pants only for warmth and zipped them over one of the two loose-fitting, long cotton pants that I wore on alternate days. One day, the tan pair; the next day, it would be the black ones. It was my habit to wash out the clothes worn that day while I showered at the communal facilities that were at the *refugio*s. Then I put on the other dry pants and one of the shirts to sleep in. In the morning, I was already dressed, although very rumpled, for that day's walk.

The cotton sleeveless top I brought with me I used only as an undershirt. To wear it in the sun would mean certain serious sunburn within an hour or two. I didn't want to have a reason like that keep me from continuing. Getting badly sunburned was something that was controllable. At the *refugio* in Zubiri, where I stayed the night before getting to Pamplona, there was a woman who had to end her walk because she was so badly sunburned. She had been walking in a halter top with no hat.

For warmth I had a cotton lightweight sweatshirt with a hood and a zippered windbreaker jacket. It was good to have them both when I slept at night and in the early mornings in the mountains, but not on the days that scorched the ground, as well as my eyes, my skin, and my throat.

The overcast skies brought with them the threat of showers. I hoped they'd hold off as I looked out at the treeless fields of wheat.

After clearing
the sprawl to the
west of Pamplona,
the *Sierra del Perdón*
loomed ahead of me beyond the
wheat fields. For two full days,
even before reaching the city,
I had been looking at the
mountain in the distance.

The fields were endless and in fact, they were all you could see for miles ahead. If it did start to rain, there'd be nowhere to get shelter until I reached the village I could just make out halfway up the mountain.

I put the water bottle away and searched for my rain poncho, tucked it into a more accessible outside pocket, made some adjustments to my pack then hoisted it up and onto my back again. My body slumped with the weight. In time, I knew I'd get stronger. *Let's go, Grace. Onward and upward!*

"Look, you've just got to try harder!" I screamed as we sat in the car. Grace had never looked so cowed. I surprised myself.

Three months had gone into looking for a nursing home for her. I had visited some depressing places that were crowded with (mostly) women all sitting in wheel chairs lining the hallways, staring off at nothing. Others were numbly shuffling along with walkers in the corridors of the grim and smelly hospital-like places—thirty-eight in all. None were great. Given Grace's lack of money to pay for something more pleasant in an assisted living home, she'd have to live where Medicare residents were accepted. There wasn't much to choose from.

One of the nursing homes seemed what I considered "good." It was in a neighborhood of trees and private homes just outside of Boston and would be relatively convenient for me to visit her. The common rooms were cheerful and the halls had paintings hanging on brightly colored walls instead of the line-up of wheel chair bound ladies. So I completed all the paper work, gave notice to the manager of the apartment building where Grace lived and went about making plans to clear out her furniture and household things.

The day came for me to drive her with the few belongings she was permitted to bring with her to the home. I had a terrible feeling about the move, even though I was trying to be optimistic: *It'll be better for her. She'll have people around her to look after her and she'll maybe make some friends and have things to do besides just sitting in her apartment by herself.*

Clearly Grace was not able to live alone without a lot of help—my help—which had become overwhelming. Cleaning her apartment, doing her laundry, dishes, shopping, taking her to doctor's appointments for the past three years had started to take its toll on me. I was exhausted by handling my own home, design business, and what social life I could fit into the mix. She was losing her balance and refused to use a cane to steady herself. One evening I found her on the floor of her apartment, where she had been lying for several hours; another time she was there for a full day. She refused to wear an alarm-system necklace where she might have alerted someone that she needed help and she was embarrassed to pull a cord available in her bathroom because she didn't want anyone to find her nude.

We drove out to the home, I parked next to the sidewalk in front of the single-story building and walked Grace up the path to the front door. I had her suitcase in one hand and all of the papers and documents I was told to bring in the other. As we slowly walked toward the door, I was chattering on about how lovely it all was. "Oh, look at that flowering tree," I said. "I didn't realize you can see the water from here. We can go for walks in the neighborhood when I come visit."

The "welcome" desk was straight ahead of us and the woman I had spoken with when I visited before stepped out and grasped Grace's hand.

"Well, you must be Grace! How nice to meet you, Hon. Welcome, welcome. My name is Suzie!" she bubbled. "Let's see, do we have all of our things? Good, good." she looked down as I indicated the suitcase next to me. "Let's go directly to our new room and put all of our things there and then we'll all go on a little walking tour. 'kay, Hon? I think there's a crafts class going on right now. Your daughter tells me you like doing crafty things. Well, isn't that just wonderful. Yeah."

Grace was numbed by it all. She seemed so vulnerable and complacent, as if she had given up and was just going to do as she was told. I liked her better when she was angry and belligerent. We walked a short distance from the desk to a room where the door was propped open with a chair and the woman pointed to a bed in the corner. The room was crammed with six, or maybe eight beds, each with its own bedside table and chair along side it. There was one shared bathroom at the opposite end of the room. Curtains that hung between the beds for privacy were pushed back against the walls. Two windows brought little daylight into the shady side of the building. "Well, here we are Grace! This will be our new little home," Suzie said as she patted the mattress on the neatly made up bed.

Something inside of me just said *NO!* I couldn't leave her there. I thanked the woman for her time and said I'd changed my mind. Grace wouldn't be staying. As I took Grace's arm and walked her as quickly as she could move past the front desk, I grabbed the envelope of papers I had brought with us and made for the door. When we got to the car, it was clear that Grace was very confused. I tried to explain.

"If you'd just try a little harder to keep yourself clean!" I pleaded "If you'd try a little harder to keep your apartment neater. If you'd just take your medicine and wear a diaper-thing to bed so it wouldn't be so soaked and smelly! If you'd just use a cane to get around when you're feeling dizzy! If you'd just wear one of those alarm systems around your neck. Please, Mom, please! I just can't leave you in a place like that! We can do this if you'd only try a little harder to help." I reasoned. "We'll get back to the apartment right away and I'll let them know you're staying."

She did try a little harder—for a while. At least she had one more year of independence before ultimately having to make that move. I had more time to find a better place.

Looking behind me from the rise I'd reached, I could see all of Pamplona below stretching out across the valley basin. The Arga River meanders through the valley, flanked by orchards and groves of olive and fruit trees. There's a succession of bridges crossing it, some of them medieval and certainly there when the early pilgrims crossed over to climb this mountain. On the other side of the river are the city's last major suburbs below *Mount San Cristobál*, the mountain to the north of Pamplona.

What I knew about Pamplona had to do with Ernest Hemingway's description of bullfights and the annual running of the bulls. There's a bust of Hemingway that stands just outside the famous bull ring in a small park. It has a plaque that commemorates his pleasure and patronage of the Pamplona bullfights. It's remarkable for its ugliness and for it memorializing an American and not one of Spain's own great patriots and lovers of bullfights.

The festival that occasions the bulls running through the streets happens every July. It's an event many flock to see, but I was glad I wasn't walking through Pamplona when the bulls were. During the *Fiesta de San Fermín*, which includes daily dispatches of running bulls, there are thousands of tourists that descend on the city. Processions of "giants" and *cabezudos* (*papier maché* figures with large heads), fireworks, and dancing in the streets make it a favorite national festival. It begins around the 6th of July with a rocket launched from the City Hall and a party goes on for nine days and nights thereafter. Each morning of the

Fiesta, at eight o'clock, six bulls are released from a corral to run a half-mile course through the City Hall square, past the *Calle Mercaderes* and finally down the *Calle Estafeta*, the heart of the festival activities, to the bull ring where they take part in the afternoon bullfight.

Of the hundreds of young men (and increasingly, women) who run in front of and alongside the bulls, many of them are injured and on occasion, there have been some deaths. After being whipped into a frenzy by prodding and goading them as they run "free" down the narrow streets, the bulls are then herded into the bullring for that bizarre dance of death.

There are a lot of new buildings in Pamplona and the architecture is strong and bold with a massiveness that reflects the traditional Basque large, simple building styles. There are new apartments, and civic buildings as well, and they all seem to carry the Spanish flare for the dramatic. There's a lot of energy and excitement about the city—a sense of prosperity in this, the geographical and cultural center of the province of Navarra. The mix of the old and the new sit comfortably together. Vast medieval walls that serpentine around the city stand next to contemporary buildings that champion the new direction for all of Spain. I felt very uplifted by it.

After descending the Pyrenees, the Camino enters Pamplona below the city's ramparts, circling the city briefly before rising to an impressive, stone entrance at the north, the *Portal de Francia*. Entering the gateway with its monumental walls, covered in the patina of millennium, you can almost feel the presence of the pilgrims who walked this way before. As I passed through the ancient stone wall, I got a sense that I'd reached an important point on the journey. The open door of the city foretold of nourishment, rest, and camaraderie. Kings and Queens, paupers and the wealthy, the firm and the infirm would have entered here on the way to Santiago, no doubt seeking the refuge that pilgrims still look forward to today.

The usual cement posts marked with a scallop shell or the painted wide yellow arrows that define the path in the countryside were gone. Sometimes, if you're watching closely, you can find a shell painted on the side of a building or a ceramic tile depicting a shell imbedded in the facade of a house, but you can miss them, too. So the trail became indistinguishable to me in the maze of streets and small alleyways. It was actually easier to spot another pilgrim than to see the trail markers so I decided to follow a couple of them, assuming that since it was late afternoon, they were probably heading for the main *refugio* for the night.

I had covered about thirteen miles that day and walked for a longer number of hours than I had intended. I hoped there'd be a bed left for me there; otherwise, I'd have to walk out of Pamplona another three miles to the next *refugio*. Even one more mile seemed a daunting idea, let alone three. The alternative would have been to take a room in a hotel which was not even a consideration. I wanted an "authentic" experience as a pilgrim.

Fortunately, I spotted the *Calle Ansoleaga*, the street where I knew to look for the *refugio*. It was listed on the sheets that served as my ersatz guidebook. Many pilgrims were sitting around outside the narrow, ancient building on the corner of the small street. I arrived in time to take the last bunkbed available that night. After showing my Pilgrim's Passport, getting it stamped, signing in, and paying my few euros, I claimed the bed and took off my pack for the last time that day.

The shower had been creatively built into one of the two small bathrooms both of which took a piece out of the staircase. For the thirty beds that were on the two upper floors of the building, that one shower stall was well used for a couple of hours every afternoon. There was no hot water left when I turned on the tap but I relished washing away the day's grit from my hair, my face, and body anyhow. My feet cooled in the puddle that began to form in the bottom of the stall.

Changing into clean clothes, I washed out my dirty ones, and hung them indoors on ropes someone had strung around the bathroom, hoping they'd be dry enough before I left early the next day. Many people walk out from *refugio*s in the mornings with their laundry—shirts, underclothes, and socks—tied to the outside of their backpacks, drying as they walk.

"*Hola!*" I said as I entered the small kitchen where other pilgrims were cooking. I recognized the three Mexican Boy Scouts who always walked in full dress uniform—bright red shirts, dark blue pants with scarf and bolo, including a full array of merit badges. They were older than what we think of as Boy Scouts in the States—probably around eighteen or nineteen.

The day before, I saw them tending to a group of walkers with their salve for badly blistered feet. They had stopped in their rapid pace on the descent through the mountains to administer their services. The rocks were jutting up out of the hillside on edge and it was very difficult to navigate those edges. One otherwise healthy young man, walking in simple, low-cut Nikes, had to end his walk after his first day because the soles of his feet had become so badly bruised by the knife-like edges of those rocks. Laying on his bunk bed, in the *refugio* at Zubiri, with his red and grotesquely swollen feet hanging over the end of the bed, he told me he'd try again next year—with better walking shoes. He was still in bed when I left in the morning. Word traveled that later that day the overseer of the *refugio* had called an ambulance to take him to a clinic—the swelling had gotten worse.

The Scouts all sang out in a chorus of *"Hola, señora!"* as I put my groceries down on a table near the stove. They were all speaking Spanish with a woman I learned was from San Salvador. She was cooking a delicious-smelling chili dinner of sausage and beans and tomatoes for all of them and their chatter stopped only to offer me a seat and some Coke to drink.

I declined both the seat and the Coke and began to look for a corkscrew to open the cold bottle of white Rioja wine I had just bought at the market in the square below. I had been longing for a glass of wine from the famous province I'd be entering in a few days. In fact, I wasn't as hungry for the bread and cheese I bought as I was for the wine.

There was an array of different glasses and mugs in the cabinet over the sink. While the others went back to their chatter, I poured us all some wine and raised a toast. *"Ultreya!"* I said, and they returned with raised glasses, *"Gracias, señora, Buen Camino!"*

We were barely able to understand one another, but we all spoke slowly and loud—with many gestures—and filled our glasses again. We told our now well-practiced stories of why we were there and how we had gotten there. I didn't understand much of the story from the Scouts, one of them, Marco, spoke a little English and he was pressed into interpreting for us all. I think they were definitely going to get a merit badge if they made it all the way to Santiago—and well deserved it would be. The woman from San Salvador was walking for her mother. I'm not sure why. Was she dying? Did she already die? I swallowed the last of my wine, offered the rest of my bread and cheese to the others and said *"Buenas noches."* The woman stood and went to the stove to ladle the steaming fragrant chili into bowls.

In the morning I searched out a cafe where I could get a cup of Spanish coffee, the delicious *café con leché*, with its hot foamy top served in very large cups. That, along with a *tortilla de patata* (made with eggs and chunks of potatoes) would give me energy for several hours. I had enjoyed the *tortilla* so much the morning before in Larrasoaña, that I had ordered two of them.

Before leaving Pamplona, I wanted to be sure to see the cathedral so I followed the sound of the bells that had just begun tolling as I stepped out of the cafe. After making a few turns down short alleyways, I came to an open square where the imposing Santa María Cathedral stands.

"...but, *señorita*, I don't have any interest in visiting the museum, I just want to see the cathedral. Are you saying I have to pay to enter the church?" The slim and scruffy looking elderly man with an Australian accent leaned on his walking stick as he addressed the trim young woman who was selling tickets inside the door. I stood behind him in line as he tried to negotiate with the woman.

This man was one of many who objected to having to pay to enter some of the churches along the Camino. Most pilgrims were willing to pay to visit museums and other historic civic buildings, but the majority who were walking for religious or even non-religious reasons, felt that the churches should be open and free to all.

"Yes, sir, I'm very sorry but to enter you must buy a ticket which will give you entrance to the cloister, the cathedral and the museum," she responded in perfect English. "The fee covers a great many costs that we have in maintaining the cathedral for the pilgrims, like yourself, who want to come through. Sometimes we have thousands in one week."

"Alright then. I won't be going in. Good day to you." he said as he hobbled out through the massive wooden door. He had a small pack on his back with a blanket roll tied on with bits of rope. His thin and wiry frame was bent over a rustic, hand-hewn walking stick. Long gray wisps of his hair were entangled with his beard which hung down on his chest in matted clumps. The fatigue that showed in his body was evidence that he had walked a long way. The stars were most likely his *refugio.* There was no money for entrance fees in those slim pockets. The "fee" situation will, no doubt, have to be resolved. Many people spoke of it all along the path.

I, however, paid the *señorita* my entrance fee, took the ticket and my "complimentary" visitor's guide, and went into the church. The cathedral was originally a Roman building but what's there today was built in 1394 with an 18th century facade. The plan is simple with a central nave and a transept, high pointed Gothic arches and windows with clear glass that let in more light than one would expect in a building of this period. The tomb of Carlos III the Noble and his wife Leonor is in the central nave. With the recumbent figures of the two monarchs, the tomb is a wonderful example of the sober Spanish Gothic sculpture of the 15th century. There's an altar piece of Saint Thomas that was interesting, too. I stopped to do a few sketches of some pieces I liked.

In keeping with my decision to light a candle when I stopped in churches along the way—in thanks for safe passage, or for Grace's well being in the after world or just for the ceremony of it—before leaving I turned to a side altar where it looked like candles were burning and chose one to light myself. It was amusing to see that the people in charge of business matters at the cathedral had thought about the consumption of candles, too. Rather than wastefully using wax candles, there were small lights on the ends of plain white columns and a box to insert a one euro coin. One coin turned on two lights—for a period of time. My coin turned on three. A bonus day.

From the cathedral there's an entrance into the cloister through the *Puerta del Amparo*, a large Gothic door with a sculpture of the Virgin Mary in the space over the door. The beautiful, airy cloister is very fine high Gothic in style and it's decorated with early carved wooden sculptures of saints and the Madonna and child. Most of the carvings are brightly painted and gilded and they show the "child" as just that—not a babe in arms, at his mother's breast but a three- or four-year old, sitting upright on his mother's lap. Very different from the Italian Madonnas of the same period where the baby is clearly adored, lying wrapped in his mother's arms.

A large school group arrived to tour the museum. I decided to avoid the noise and get back on the path. Puente la Reina was my goal before stopping for the night—more than fifteen miles ahead.

For in their hearts doth Nature stir them so
Then people long on pilgrimage to go
And palmers to be seeking foreign strands
To distant shrines renowned in sundry lands.

Geoffrey Chaucer

After clearing the sprawl to the west of Pamplona, the *Sierra del Perdón* loomed ahead of me beyond the wheat fields. For two full days, even before reaching the city, I had been looking at the mountain in the distance. Its spine runs north and southeast creating a protective arm around Pamplona, almost seeming to shield the beautiful city from whatever might invade her from the west.

The Moors were only slowed, however, in winning ancient *"Pompaelo"* by the presence of this huge wall of a mountain. The Roman general, Pompey, is said to have named the city and there's a bust of him in the historic center on the *Avenida de Bayona*. By 718 AD Pamplona served as the northern frontier of the Islamic territory that stretched from northern Africa and throughout the Iberian peninsula. The people of the city were constrained to fight in many skirmishes against the Franks. Because of these on-going battles, in 778, Charlemagne destroyed the city walls of Pamplona as he retreated from defeat in the Battle of Roncevaux Pass. He left his general and closest friend, Roland, in charge of the rearguard as he went off to news of trouble back home in Saxony.

It was during Roland's withdrawal that the rearguard was ambushed and Roland was killed in a valley near Roncesvalles. Close to the settlement in Roncesvalles there's a large, broken, grey boulder with pink veins running through it. Roland was supposed to have struck his sword on that rock and broke the stone but not his magical sword.

The climb was slow and gradual up the side of the mountain. The wide dirt and gravel path took me through beautiful wheat fields that bent in the breeze that was picking up. I began to think about Grace again. I wondered how she'd feel about my going all this way to leave her ashes. My brother thought she would have liked the adventure and he was grateful that I was willing to give her a "final resting place." She had died the year before, after withering in a nursing home for her last few years. She was cremated because, thankfully, she said that's what she wanted. Beyond that though, there were no plans. I don't remember a day in the last twelve years that I had been looking after her that she didn't wish the struggle were over. But what was to come next was a topic of little interest to her.

I kept her ashes on the floor of my bedroom closet, still in the container I was given at the crematorium when I went to pick them up. "Here's your dear mother, Grace, Ms. Lauran," said the heavy-set funeral director with soft round hands. He was sweating in his tight-fitting black suit as he handed me a black paper shopping bag with a white lily printed on one side. Inside the bag was a perfectly wrapped brown paper parcel that looked like it only needed a few stamps to be sent on its way. I signed some papers. He gave me copies of her death certificate, and I carried her out to the car. *Front seat or back?* I wondered.

I disagreed with my brother's take on her possibly liking this adventure. She was too afraid of things and too uncomfortable with herself. Her discomfort, her unhappiness, and yes, her fury made my brother and me both protective and yet, always fearful of her.

The *Sierra del Perdón* serves as a platform for many windmills, as well as a variety of radio towers and other antennae. The Spanish have taken to windmills for energy very seriously. The very tall, thin white columns with their three spinning blades create a droning strum that's quite loud when you get near them. They stand as sentinels on almost every mountain in the northern provinces. Another pilgrim told me that Spain's windmills provide five percent of the energy needs of the country and that the government-run, Eolic Wind Power Company has plans to double that over the next five years.

This was the first mountain on the path that had to be climbed up and over. In the Pyrenees the path generally descends from Roncesvalles. The Camino follows mountain passes and valleys through and around the highest peaks. There was no way around this *sierra*, however. It was a blessing to not have full sun as I began my ascent.

Drizzling rain began just as I started the climb. It was cool and refreshing but it was clear I'd soon be very wet if I didn't stop and put on my poncho. I took off my hat once more and laid it aside while I reached around to the side pocket of my backpack where I had put the poncho earlier. Throwing it over my backpack and myself would hopefully keep everything dry. After wrestling with the grommets that held the sides together, I put my hat back on over of the hood of the poncho to keep the rain out of my eyes, and continued walking.

The wheat fields cover the entire base of this side of the mountain; running almost to the garden plots that lie outside of the small village now just ahead on the path. It was three hours before I reached Zariquiegui where I stopped to rest, took off my pack, and filled my water bottle at the fountain in the square. The town looked deserted except for a few doves fluttering around the nearby chapel. The outer walls of the chapel served as a community news board with ten or so pieces of paper attached there fluttering in the breeze broadcasting events to come. A car pulled up to a small house behind me, and as I turned I saw a man wearing tattered farm clothes and a wide brimmed hat get out of the car and briskly enter the house, carrying a long thin loaf of French-style bread under his arm.

A stone slab that was still wet from the rain served as a seat. I dug in my pack to find the apple I had bought with my groceries the night before in Pamplona and wished there was more to eat. Carrying the extra weight of food with me up that mountain would have been a mistake, but the climb made me ravenous. Soon I'd have to find an open market or a cafe where I could get something to eat.

I wandered through the village streets; following the Camino trail markers, past shuttered shops and houses and out to continue the more pronounced ascent of the *sierra*. The light rain had let up a little as I followed the path zigzagging up the side of the mountain for another two hours. There were no trees along the path only scrubby underbrush in areas that weren't planted with vegetables or vines. When the clouds parted, Pamplona shimmered in the mist below, now just a small jewel in an otherwise foggy green landscape. Ahead was the strange and melancholy strumming and whirring sound of the huge windmills standing on the crest of the mountain. It was impossible not to think of Don Quixote and his windmills. Were these my windmills? My symbols of an unnecessary adventure?

A friend of mine who's a photographer, took a picture of an orphaned girl she came across in a small town in India. It's titled, "Girl With No Mother." The shy-looking young girl stands against a crumbling wall on a dirt floor, looking wistfully away from the viewer. Her bent shoulders are the frame that supports a far-too-large and tattered sweater. She has a scarf around her head, tied at the back that covers her hair and a necklace hangs over a dirty white shirt, neatly buttoned to the top. There are bracelets on both her wrists. She's wearing a dirty flowered skirt that hangs below her knees. Sandals protect her feet that emerge from branch-thin legs. She looks to be about ten-years old and has clearly made attempts to look her best. When I look at her, I'm well aware of how fortunate my life has been and yet somewhere inside of me there is the spirit of that orphaned girl.

Grace died without my ever learning why my brother and I were placed in an orphanage and lived for a time in a foster home. As the years separated us even further, what I did come to feel for her was sympathy and, for some reason, a sense of responsibility to protect her—from what? From some unspoken sense of shame that never had a name; from people treating her badly or taking advantage of her frailty. Carrying her ashes on the Camino and leaving them at the *Cruz de Ferro* I hoped would be a way for me to put her memory to rest—to leave her there and walk on. Maybe it would be a symbolic way for me to continue my life journey with a clean slate. I could only hope that it would leave me with a feeling that I had done all I could have done for her. I would be absolved from having contributed to her unhappiness.

The *Cruz de Ferro* (Iron Cross) is at the very summit of the highest mountain on the Camino, *Mount Irago*. It's a very emblematic monument of the Camino—just a simple iron cross set in a long wooden trunk that is planted in a *milladoiro*, a huge mound of stones. These stones (and many shells as well) have been left by pilgrims for over a thousand years. They represent prayers for safe passage, for the return of health, for blessings received or hoped for, or burdens left behind, with grati-tude. The mountain is beyond Rabanal in the province of León, almost three hundred miles away.

When I imagine her standing in front of me, I see only the sadness Grace carried in her eyes and in her whole way of being. She had an uncontrollable anger and would fly into a rage at quite unexpected times and with little provocation. I often wonder how different her life might have been were it to have been more acceptable in her time and in her culture to get psychological help. The anger was a clinical problem as I came to learn many years later, and it didn't subside very readily.

When Grace was angry, the anger, or rage really, lasted for days and her wild screaming echoed through the house for hours. My brother and I were usually hiding-out in our rooms. He would be reading or building an airplane model, and I would be drawing or playing with my dolls. Both of us hoping not to say or do anything that would ignite her. I shudder even now with the memory of the terror I felt when I thought she was coming after me. Staying clear of her stinging hands was a preoccupation of mine. When I'd hide under my bed, she'd find me and jab a broomstick wildly at me, determined to root-out a major cause of her unhappiness and possibly rid herself of it forever. Later, when she'd left, my brother whispered through my closed door, "Are you alright?"

Sitting in his favorite armchair, my father continued quietly reading. He never spoke up or protected me. Could the prescription for pare-goric, an opium derivative, that he kept available to her, have been his way of helping? He would put his book down or turn down a corner of the paper he was reading to look in her direction. "Now, Grace, calm down, dear," he'd offer as her anger escalated.

Reaching the summit, I stopped to rest on a bench and take my poncho and backpack off. Although it was misty, there was no rain and I needed some air. My shirt was soaked with sweat and sticking to me. There were picnic tables and seats, a stone boulder held a plaque—something commemorative about the Camino, no doubt. I couldn't read the Spanish inscription. The Eolic Wind Power Company had commis-sioned a life size statue of a group of pilgrims walking in line, which was set just at the crest of the mountain. It had a quality to it like Rodin's "Burghers of Calais," a melancholy group wandering together.

There was a man at the summit who had just pulled off the road into the rest area and was standing next to his VW camper van. He was round and florid and seemed cheerful. He was speaking an almost cockney English, very loudly to two other pilgrims—describing the walk ahead. I learned that he's called "The Savior of the Camino." He travels from one end of the Camino to the other with his van of remedies and refreshments offering cold drinks, hot coffee or tea, cookies, aspirins, and blister plasters, all for a donation. He also administered some basic first aid to a pilgrim in the time that I was there resting. Just a simple wrap around a knee that had gotten scraped but much appreciated by the pilgrim. He was available to drive to a local hospital or clinic if the climb was overly strenuous for anyone.

"What say, deary, have a little biscuit?" he said as he approached me, "You're lookin' rather tuckered, hey? Good day for the climb though. Don't want too much sun coming up that mountain!"

I accepted his offer of the cookie and chatted with him for a while. He's now a "pensioner" with time on his hands.

"Quite a time, hey? Biggest adven'cha' I ever had! Walked the Camino, oh, 'bout five years ago. Had such a grand time of it, decided to spend half a year drivin' the length of the thing; stopping this place an 'tuther, higgledy-piggledy, wherever the path crosses the road-way," he explained.

He enjoyed the camaraderie with the pilgrims and liked to think he was helping them on their way. The donations kept him in gas for the van in which he slept. Sometimes he could buy his stash of remedies with the money that was left. For the other half of the year—the winter—he drove to the southern coast, to a town near Malaga where he rents an inexpensive apartment and "just wiggles the toes a bit."

The Savior was called away to tend to blisters on a walker who had hobbled into view at the summit just as a small, private mini-bus turned off the road. All the doors opened at once and outpoured a var-ied group, young and old. They looked the most refreshed of anyone standing there gazing out over the vast sea of mountaintops piercing the shroud of clouds below. They were being driven along the Camino

with a guide, stopping at points where they could see an extended part of the "Way" and maybe encounter some actual pilgrims.

The guide was speaking in heavily accented English, telling her bus load of travelers about the significance of this point on the Camino and talking about the sculpture and the artist who made it. She also told them about the miracle of the *Fuente Reniega* (Fountain of Renouncement) that took place just below the summit. It was difficult to understand all she was saying but it seemed that the miracle had to do with the Devil tempting a thirsty pilgrim. If he would renounce his faith, the Devil would give him water. Refusing to be tempted, he was visited by Santiago who led the devout pilgrim to this now dry spring. There are a lot of places along the Camino where miracles took place. This one might just as easily have been the miracle of having reached the top of the *Sierra del Perdón*.

Prompted by The Savior, some of the touring group wandered over to where I was sitting and asked me more about why I was walking. Their attentions made me uncomfortable.

"How could you be walking this alone?" asked a young woman, incredulous at the mere thought. "Aren't you afraid by yourself?" Her eyebrows raised in astonishment. "How fast do you have to walk? I mean, how many miles a day do you have to walk to make it to Santiago in the time you have?"

"Fear hasn't been a factor in my plans. If I started getting fearful then all I'd see would be things to be afraid of. The path takes you along at whatever pace you want to go," I responded, "and mine is that of a snail, compared to a lot of walkers! I'm hoping to make about twelve to fifteen miles a day—more when I can."

"Wow. That's a lot of walking with that backpack! What's it been like to walk just this part? I mean from Roncesvalles?" asked a well-dressed middle-aged man. "Do you think you'll really make it all the way to Santiago de Compostela?"

"Well, it's like walking anywhere else, I suppose, except you're doing more of it than usual! I can't possibly know yet what it'll be like further on. Some people say the stretch from Roncesvalles is supposed to be the hardest part—through the Pyrenees, that is. Other people have told me it's difficult in the mountains after Astorga. I guess I'll see about that. More than four hundred and fifty miles to go! I can only hope I'll make it."

They confessed to being very comfortable in the mini-bus that took them nightly to charming *pensionés* where they slept and ate very well. They would be driving on to Puente la Reina to have lunch before heading toward Navarette for the evening. I wouldn't make it to Navarette for at least three more days.

The Italian brothers from Pordenone I had met at Roncesvalles on the first night arrived and I chatted with them for a while. They were moving on quickly to try to catch-up with some friends who left Pamplona earlier that morning. Maybe I'd see them at Puente la Reina later that day.

After gathering my things together and re-arranging my backpack, a constant activity, I put my poncho back in the outside pocket, within reach, if it started to rain again. I hoisted on the pack and walked over to say good-bye to The Savior.

"Well, now, you take care, deary! I'll be keepin' my eye out for ya' as I go along—I mean, you and your mum—and I'll be askin' others if they've seen ya'. Just incase you take a fall or somethin'—I'll be lookin' for ya'! *Buen Camino! Ultreya!*"

"Thanks," I called out as I waved and crossed the road to find the path. *"Buen Camino!"*

Certainly the gray day and my memories of Grace hadn't helped my mood but I was hungry and so I set off to find something good for lunch. The Savior told me there was a bar in a small town a few miles ahead. It was likely to be open and he recommended their *sopa zarauztarra*, a Basque traditional soup made from roasted rice. He said the fragrance of garlic is powerful and you can keep flies off of you for days with only one bowl full. After leaving Navarra in a couple of days, Basque dishes would be a rarity in local bars, so with the thought of the hot fragrant soup in mind, I began to follow the path as it wandered down the slope and on to Santiago.

Don't worry about saving these songs!
And if one of our instruments breaks,
    it doesn't matter.
We have fallen into the place
    where everything is music.

Rumi

More than an hour had passed since leaving the windmills when I entered a small village that, once again, looked shuttered and deserted. Continuing to follow the scallop shell markers and *las flechas de amarillas*, the wide yellow arrows painted on the curbs that had become more common, I rounded a bend in the cobbled road and saw a sign for a bar.

Several backpacks and walking sticks were piled-up outside the entrance, sheltered from the drizzle. The building was new, very low and modern looking. It was set back from the road with an empty patio in the area at the front. Round metal tables were randomly placed on the pebble-strewn earth with a few young trees planted to offer shade. White plastic chairs stacked in three columns were lined-up near the door. A nice setting in good weather, no doubt. As I opened the door, the atmosphere spilled out in waves of laughter and conversation, dishes clanging, the fragrance of spices, warm breads and cigarettes, the sounds of a sizzling grille.

Not trusting to leave my backpack idle outside with the others, I struggled out of it at the entrance and greeted the woman standing near the cash register. She wiped her brow with a swipe of her fore-arm and nervously looked around the restaurant to see a way to fit me

44

into the boisterous crowd they had for lunch. My backpack stood balanced against the wall under a coat rack next to the door.

I nodded and waved *"Hola"* to a few people I recognized from the last few days on the path. There was The Dutch Couple Who Picnic—the rain must have driven them indoors. It seemed that even though they'd be sitting on a blanket in a field, having lunch in one place, there they'd be, waving to me, having another picnic later on that same day. There were The Singing Señoritas who drank heavily at night and still rose to sing to everyone in the morning. *"Coo-ba, Coo-ba, libre C O-O-O-O ba!"* They were sharing a table with a group of four local boys who were entranced by the two pretty women. Laughter rolled around their table.

I asked for a large bottle of water and settled onto a stool at the bar. The garlic-flavored rice soup that was to spare me the flies had been consumed by the time I arrived so I ordered a *plato combinado* which the waiter pointed out on a table nearby. It looked very appetizing with grilled fish, chunks of roasted potatoes (*patatas asado*), beans (*judias*) and a green salad. The plate arrived quickly with good crusty bread, and the eye of the fish watching me. Two cups of frothy coffee and a slice of rich sweet cake (*tarta dolce*) completed my rare mid-day feast.

Before leaving I took advantage of the hot water and soap in the restroom to wash some of the day's grit from my face and neck. Looking at my hair and face in the mirror over the sink, I put on some more sun-protectant that was in a pouch at my waist, and made a note that it was a good thing not to see a mirror very often.

I felt clean, well fed, and fully refreshed as I went out into the restaurant again. I waved and said *"Buen Camino,"* to those pilgrims who looked up from their plates and raised a hand to say good-bye. The man behind the counter called out to the woman at the cash register, and I paid whatever amount she decreed. Bending down to lift my backpack, I took a deep breath and supported the weight with my knee as I slipped an arm through a strap and turned to catch the other one, tipping forward to settle the bag high on my back. I adjusted the straps and belt to accommodate my full stomach, staggered with the weight for a minute, and continued out the door.

Mist was rising from the damp pavement. The spattering and intermittent drizzle had stopped and the air had cleared a little, making the afternoon ahead look more promising. The sun dappled the patio with patches of warmth where it filtered through the shade trees. I walked to the end of the pathway and turned left to find the markers again. If I was to make it to Puente La Reina that afternoon, I had to pick up my pace.

"Hola! Hola, señora! Hola!" the crunching sound of hurrying boots came from behind me just as I left the roadway to follow the path. Turning to see who was calling, I saw a slim and well-muscled man wearing a close-fitting blue short-sleeved shirt and jeans. He was smiling, holding on to the shoulder strap of his backpack with one hand as he hurried toward me, waving with the other. Tanned and tall with dark, close-trimmed hair and an aquiline nose, he had dark, bright eyes that showed no sign of defeat. Pointing at myself, I said, "Me?"

"Si, señora," he said breathlessly, and then he said something else. Seeing that I didn't understand, he switched to what I recognized as French. He said something more as I stood looking at him nodding my head and smiling, completely bewildered by what he was trying to tell me.

"Sprechen sie deutsche?" he offered.

"I'm American," I said. "I understand a little French and I studied Spanish in high school briefly, so I'm not very good with that either. I speak *un po d'italiano* but I'm much better in English."

"Oh, *si, si,* I understand. We speak the English then," he smiled openly showing perfectly straight white teeth. "Is okay I walk with you, *señora*? You are alone, with no one. I am with no one also."

"Sure. I mean, great! That would be nice!" I said. I had been thinking while eating lunch that I'd enjoy having someone to talk to. My solitude was what I'd asked for but I was feeling the need for some company.

"Where are you from?" I asked as we walked on next to each other, "You speak so many languages, you could manage anywhere, I suppose."

"I am from Argentina. A very small place a little near to Buenos Aires. We have the fame because Manuel de Falla lived in there. You know who is this man, Manuel de Falla?"

"Oh, yes," I said, "I love his music. Well, that is, I know his "Nights in the Gardens of Spain" and "The Three-Cornered Hat." I think Picasso designed the sets for that ballet when it was first performed, no?" My new companion seemed genuinely pleased that his pride in de Falla was not lost on me.

"Si, si, this is right! He was good friend to my father. Yes, my father knew him well. He died at 1946, way, way before I was born," he emphasized, waving his hand over his shoulder. "He left Spain after civil war here when Franco and his people took power. Very sad. Very sad. He loved Spain very, very much."

"You, *señora?* Where in America you come from? New York, maybe? or California?"

When I told him I had been living in Washington, he seemed genuinely delighted but I was to learn that many things delighted him. He wanted to know how I felt about Bush and the war in Iraq. I told him about my profound shame at the whole thing and my horror at all the bombings and deaths. I had never been in Europe when I didn't feel a certain naive pride in being American, but not this time. Any conversation about America usually brought negative comments about the war or complete silence when people learned I was American. I apologized for my country's arrogance. He was genuinely sympathetic and assured me that "Everyone still love Americans, *señora!* But not Bush. No, no, no," he emphasized, wagging his head. "Not this man."

As we walked, we talked about our experiences on the Camino. He laughed readily as we compared the relative comforts of *refugios*. His one experience so far had been a good one. We talked about whether or not we had met some of the same pilgrims, dealing with blisters, and, the most frequently asked question, why we were walking.

"I walk for my family, *señora,* I walk to get work. I am architect but there is no work in Buenos Aires. No work in all Argentina! I have a job here in Spain, in Valencia. My family they stay in Argentina. I call them. At end of week, I telephone them always. I do building here, I make with my hands—how you call, *"construcción"*—but I am architect. I have fifty-nine years and I have no architect work."

It was clearly impossible that he was fifty-nine years old and if he was, I wanted to drink some of his water. I decided he must have the numbers wrong and, in fact, learned later that he had *thirty*-nine years. He was only ten years older than my son, Michael, and he had so much on his shoulders already. His spirit was indefatigable and the joy he showed in everything—in other people, in the fields of beautiful spring flowers around us, and in the privilege of walking this ancient path was infectious.

"Here, I show you my house I design for my family. It is in the mountains." he slid his backpack off and reached into a zippered side pocket as we stopped on the path. "I build it also—with my brother." he added. His wallet held some snapshots of his family, three children, two teens and a toddler, and a pretty dark-haired wife standing outside a glass-clad contemporary house.

"Oh, my God! That's beautiful! It must have a lot of light—and very pretty views to those mountains in the background. You've really studied architecture, haven't you?"

"Oh, *si, si*, at university I study six years and I work for the State, in Argentina, until . . . *ppffft!*" he waved his hand in the air to suggest it disappeared. "I must work again as architect. Maybe here in Spain."

The teen-aged children in the picture were clearly not his own as he would have been too young to be their father. His wife, he explained was seven years older than he and the two teenagers were twins, her's by her first marriage; the little boy was his. She had suffered a great deal he told me, in raising the twins, a boy and a girl, all by herself, and he wanted to make her life easier and happy.

As we continued walking, we talked about the work of some of the well-known architects we both knew and discussed which were our favorites. Frank Lloyd Wright's "Fallingwater" was one of the important American buildings that he knew of and we both agreed was beautiful, and revolutionary for its time. Frank Gerry's Guggenheim Museum in Bilbao was at the top of both of our lists for the most awe-inspiring, unique and beautiful. I had seen it a couple of years before—traveling with a friend, specifically to see the building. It brought tears to my eyes as I entered the majestic space and my friend let out a "whoop!" The Architect had planned to go to Bilbao, just north of where we were walking, as soon as he could take some more time from his work.

I asked if he knew Emilio Ambasz, the only Argentinian architect I knew of. Ambasz had an office in New York and was looking for a book designer a few years before. A headhunter interviewed me a couple of times but I didn't get the job. His work was very conceptual and didn't look at all like the Mies Van der Rohe, International Style my new friend's house followed.

"*Si, si*, I know this man. Many Ambasz' ideas are not builded but they are good. Very, very, how you say? Different. He use the earth and trees to cover buildings sometimes. I like very much his *Casa de Retiro Espiritual*. I see pictures of this one. It is right near to Sevilla. Here! In *Espagña!*" he said, excitedly. "Ah, another building I must visit!"

We agreed that the amount of building that was going on in Spain would suggest that he was definitely in the right place. The historic traditions that encompassed the great neoclassic buildings of Juan de Villanueva, the 18th century architect to King Carlos III, as well as the beautiful organic forms of Antonio Gaudí, mostly in Barcelona, held hope for the future of architecture in Spain. The Architect had only a few days off from work and he wanted to walk just a small part of the Camino to ask God for a job so that he too could design beautiful buildings for Spain.

After taking a train from Valencia, he had started his pilgrimage in Pamplona. Feelings of guilt dogged him because he couldn't check his email everyday to see if he might be asked to come for an interview somewhere. After receiving a "sign" though, he decided that God wanted him to make the pilgrimage and that he had made the right decision to come.

I asked him what the sign had been and he described that he had been lying in a grassy field resting the day before and, when he looked up at the sky, he saw two jet streams and one of them crossed the path of the other, creating a crucifix. He felt that was confirmation and shed tears of joy at the time. Being deeply religious and very Catholic in his beliefs, he nearly gasped when I told him I was carrying my mother's ashes.

"*Dios santo!* Here, now? With you?—on your back you have your mother? You are a saint! *Dios!*" He repeated and crossed himself. "What a good mother she was for this you want for her! *Dios mio!*" He stood stark still with his mouth open in amazement.

"No, no. That's not it at all. I'm certainly not a saint! It's more complicated than that," I protested, looking back toward him as I continued walking on. He started to walk again and soon was next to me.

"I want to leave her ashes at the *Cruz de Ferro*. If I can make it there, I'll feel that I'll have paid her one last tribute—you know 'tribute'? I mean, sort of, one last honor. She was a very unhappy person. I want to do something meaningful for her "burial," so to speak, and for myself, too. I want to come to some peace about her, her life, her death. Do you understand?" I decided not to explain any further. When I tried to explain to others who asked, my explanations just incited more questions.

He shrugged and made a small sound that seemed like assent. We walked along silently for a while, our boots crunching the stones on the dirt path. He was limping with the pain of blisters so we stopped to make adjustments to his sox and shoelaces. I had some moleskin plasters in the first aid kit that my son had given me that I passed to The Architect. I made another patch on one of my own blisters and re-bandaged a toe that had lost its nail on the first day out. The break gave me a chance to take off my backpack and rest my shoulders.

As we sat in the shade of a tree on the path, we greeted other pilgrims as they passed by. There were the five men and one woman who walked very purposefully. I called them the "Brazilian Brigade," and The Architect laughed when I mimicked their cadence after they walked on. They were all from Sao Paulo and one of them would swoon and touch his heart with both hands whenever he saw me. "Ah, beautiful lady, I love you." he would say. Always the same words in English, no doubt learned as part of his readiness for the pilgrimage, and used on many occasions.

The group would usually walk in a line formation with a bearded older man at the front, the woman (who was the tallest) in the middle and the Romeo at the end. Even though I couldn't understand a word he said, the man at the front of the line had a manner and intonation that further suggested his role as teacher and leader. As he commented on this or that as they walked, broadly gesturing with his arms, there seemed to be a ripple of enlightenment that rolled down the line with head-nodding and turns toward each other; each offering his agreement with the idea proposed. I wondered silently how long their regiment would survive before someone went AWOL.

With the rain clouds gone, the sun was hot again even though it was late afternoon. We heard the repetitive melody of a cuckoo bird coming from the woods that lined the fields we were crossing on the well-worn path. The Architect recognized two or three other bird calls and he relished identifying them for me. He didn't know the English names for some of the birds though, but I could still fully enjoy his obvious pleasure. He would often be looking skyward as he walked, stumbling as he did. His gaze was always on any activity he might see there.

The dry dirt fields all around us looked as though they had been planted with long sheets of black plastic. Row upon row of it shimmered in the sun and covered acres of land on either side of us, emitting a crinkling sound as the light breeze passed over it. It was asparagus, my companion explained. The plastic keeps the asparagus from turning green with the sun. The Spanish much prefer their asparagus white.

Puente la Reina finally came in sight. We walked the last few miles following the dirt trail that ran next to a highway with cars flying past at dizzying speeds, sending clouds of dust lifting from the path. The trail brought us down into the town near the *refugio*. Here in Puente la Reina the two main Camino routes, the *Camino Francés* and the *Camino Aragones*, join. The *Camino Aragones* comes through the Pyrenees from Oleron St. Marie in France at the Somport Pass, and winds its way northward for about 130 miles to meet and continue west with this, the *Camino Francés*, the main pilgrimage route. Pilgrims coming from Arles and LePuy in southern France still follow the *Aragones* to make their pilgrimage to Santiago.

Puente la Reina (Queen's Bridge) is a one-street village, which is common along the Camino. The 11th century bridge that spans the River Arga is well known not only for its age but also as an outstanding example of fine medieval stonework and engineering. It was built especially for the pilgrims on the order of the deeply religious wife of Sancho El Mayor, a king of Navarra, and is still used for foot traffic by the people of the town as well as pilgrims. The queen had it built principally to help the pilgrims traveling to Santiago.

The miles had gone by quickly with our occasional talks but we were relieved to have arrived at the newly renovated *refugio* on the outskirts of town. It's run by the *Padres Reparadores*, and their monastery is nearby. The brothers are said to appear only in the morning, after all pilgrims are required to have left. They open again at noon for the next evening's visitors. Since it was almost five o'clock, there was a chance that there wouldn't be any beds left. Most pilgrims try to reach a hostel early in the afternoon, not only to avoid the heat of the day but also to be sure of finding a place to sleep. When there are no beds left, there's sometimes at least a sheltered place to roll out a sleeping bag or a field nearby to set up a tent to camp and always a place to take a shower and do some laundry. Even though people who walk are always given preferential treatment in bed assignments, after a certain hour, the beds and resting spots go to cyclists, or people on horseback. Those who drive a car aren't welcome at the *refugio*s and must find a hostel or a pension in the town.

The *Ménage á Trois* I met at dinner on my first night in Roncesvalles are an example of those who took advantage of the system. I would often see the two sisters walking together, smiling and waving to others but I never saw the husband on the path. He would, however, always be at the *refugio*s. One day I happened to see him retrieving a backpack from the trunk of a car, putting it on and walking out to meet his ladies at the door of a *refugio*.

Fortunately, there were still beds available but they were in different parts of the long two-story, stone building. The facilities were the nicest I had seen so far. There was a large open room with tables and chairs, a kitchen in the corner and some counter space for preparing meals. A bulletin board was mounted in the front hall where pilgrims could leave messages for others and find information about the path ahead. There was even a coffee vending machine that offered varieties of espresso coffee, for a one euro coin.

After signing in, stamping our Pilgrim's Passports, and putting our few euros in the locked tin provided, we parted to find the beds. I hoped to find one that wasn't a top bunk. They were the last to be taken and I didn't enjoy climbing up to one at the end of the day with the fatigue of many miles behind me. The Architect and I made plans to meet again to shop for food for dinner after we got our packs off, got showered, and had done our laundry. We were both anxious to see the famous bridge.

The dark thought, the shame, the malice,
Greet them at the door laughing,
    and invite them in.
Be grateful for whoever comes,
Because each has been sent
    as a guide from beyond.

Rumi

Walking through the aisles of the *supermercado*, it was clear that the size of the store and the wide variety of foods available was not being marketed to this town of two thousand people. The other shoppers were mostly pilgrims tasting new cheeses, choosing bottles of wine unavailable back home and taking obvious pleasure in finding products that they did have at home. There was English Stilton, Dutch Gouda and even some French and Italian wines.

The Architect guided me through the aisles and made selections for himself while explaining what was in some of the canned foods I was interested in. He told me how he would fix a delicious *salsa* for our dinner using some peppers he had picked out. He was astounded by the prices and said he didn't think the local people shopped there at all. He got some cooked meats and cheese for a *bocadillo* (sandwich) he would make for his dinner that night and maybe, if there was enough left, he'd have something for lunch the next day. I selected a couple of oranges, two bananas, two tomatoes and a dozen figs as well as canned tuna, and two cups of yogurt. There were crusty loaves of bread and rolls that looked delicious, if not morning-fresh, so I got several hard rolls for dinner, and maybe breakfast and lunch the next day.

We had decided to buy coffee from the coin-operated machine we noticed at the *refugio* and not stop in the morning until we'd covered a few miles. The crusty rolls would be nice to have with our coffee. Large bottles of water and some local wine for our dinner weighed our grocery bags down as we made our way back to the *refugio*.

We had not been carrying enough water that day and we didn't want to become dehydrated in the intense heat that was expected. The added weight of liter-sized water bottles was difficult for me to add to my pack, so I always ran the risk of running out of water. The Architect said that he would carry my water for me in his pack, so I accepted his offer and bought two big bottles. Earlier that day, he had helped me lift my backpack on after we had taken a rest and he was shocked by the weight.

"*Dio, santo, señora!*" he shouted "How many mothers you carry in there? She was very big woman, this mother of yours, no?"

I laughed and explained, "Well, no, not in the end. Not at ninety-one years. She had been very overweight when she was younger, but not when she died. She was quite small and frail. It's amazing though, huh? Here, feel how heavy this box is!" I reached into my pack and handed him the black plastic block-shaped container of Grace's ashes.

"Whew! This is much too heavy for you, *señora*! Tomorrow I carry Grace. We change—sometimes you carry Grace, sometimes you carry water," he offered.

"No," I responded, shaking my head "Thanks very much. That's nice of you but I want to carry Grace all by myself. If you carry the water, that'll be a big help."

"Oh, *si, si,* I understand. Excuse me, please, *señora*. I help with the water. You help with Grace."

In the kitchen at the *refugio* there were many pilgrims we hadn't seen before. Some could have come through the Somport Pass on the *Aragones*. We might well be seeing them more often from that point on. Since people walk at different speeds, and take side trips to visit other towns or monasteries, or rest in a town at a hostel or hotel for a day or two sometimes, there's no guarantee that anyone you meet, you'll ever see again.

I had already lost track of The Irish Priest who was part of my first Camino experience in Roncesvalles and of Demetri, the Belgian social worker who was bicycling with a trailer of all he'd need to be on the road for months. He had been discouraged by the bureaucracy in his job and so he threw his fate to the wind and decided to ride his bicycle from his home in Brussels along the Camino and then south, through Portugal, and on to Gibraltar before heading home again. He had a two-wheeled trailer that attached to the back of his bicycle somehow and it carried a cook stove, a tent and camping lamp, as well as a large supply of food, pots and pans and a coffee pot. The last morning I saw him, he made me a delicious, fresh cup of coffee on the steps of the *refugio*. When I met him in Zubiri, he had already come five hundred miles.

The Architect and I found a corner of a table free where we sat down and spread out our feast. We shared our food with each other and, with many gestures and smiles, we offered it to others sitting nearby us. Most people kept their meals to themselves but The Architect enjoyed talking to the other pilgrims in the several languages he was comfortable with and sharing our food seemed to open people up. It

was infectious and others began to offer what they had. His generosity benefited us with good cheeses, more wine, a variety of fruit and delicious cookies flavored with cardamom.

People sitting near us began to mutter something I didn't understand and there was an exodus from the tables and out the door of the *refugio*. The Architect realized that the Pilgrim's Blessing was about to take place in the Church of the Crucifix, near the *refugio*. Hurrying to clean our table and put our remaining food away in our packs, we walked out with the dozen or so others making their way down the narrow cobbled street to the church.

The *Iglesia de Crucifijo* is a late Romanesque building with a main nave and transept in a Latin cross plan. It has star-shaped ribbed vaults which add a beautiful tracery to the arched passages. In the 14th century there was work done to extend the nave beyond its 12th century beginnings, and to add to the overall size of the building. Supposedly, the church was founded by the Knights Templar who also ran a hospice in a building next door.

The Knights' role as protectors of the pilgrims is legendary and there are frequent signs of their centuries-long influence along the Camino. Some churches, chapels, and hospices, now in ruins, were built by those men who dedicated themselves to serving the Christian pilgrims on their way to Jerusalem as well as those walking to Santiago. The promise of receiving God's blessing and dispensation for all past sins, as well as a new life that would be theirs, brought hundreds of thousands on this path to Santiago during the Middle Ages. Then as now, however, not all people walking to Santiago were pilgrims seeking God's redemption. The Knights Templar offered protection from the threat of bandits and the unscrupulous.

Churches in towns and villages along the way sometimes didn't have a Pilgrim's Blessing service at the end of the day so when a church did hold one, I wanted to attend. The two services that I had attended were very moving in the quiet reverence expressed, the glow of the candles on the altar and the glitter cast from the typically carved and gilded altar pieces. Not having had a Catholic up-bringing, I wasn't entirely clear about what was going on and often just watched the proceedings in awe, knowing the same words had been spoken to many thousands of pilgrims for more than a thousand years. I was touched by the faith of the devout that the words spoken and their own silent prayers would carry them in safety to Santiago. Maybe I, too, could be among the protected.

After the service, The Architect and I joined some others who walked down the main street, the *Ruã de Romereos*, to see the bridge. Midway along the street, we turned left and passed through a large stone archway in the remains of the town walls and suddenly found ourselves standing on the bridge. We walked out onto the cobbled surface and looked over the massive stone walls down to the shallow, slow flowing river below. The round cobblestones in the middle, which formed a beautiful patterned surface, were bracketed with large square paving stones down the center and along the two outer sides. The pitch of the bridge was steep, with the walls coming almost to a point at the top of the rise in the center of the span. Six graceful arches supported the entire bridge. The center of each of the supporting pillars had a small open arched space in the middle of it, which looked decorative to me, but The Architect explained that the openings actually added to the overall strength of the structure.

There's a legend about the bridge that has to do with an exotic bird that would occasionally come to the river, wet its wings and fly to a nearby statue of the Virgin to clean her with its wings. Everyone believed it was a good omen for the whole community. Townspeople today still watch for the activities of any unusual birds seen in the region.

The sun had not yet set but it was almost nine-thirty and I was very tired. The Architect agreed that we should get back to the *refugio* and prepare to leave early in the morning to avoid the heat of the day. As we entered, the stillness in the building made it obvious that many people were already asleep. A few people were lying on their bunks writing in their journals or addressing post cards. The sounds of snoring in differing pitches and rhythms rose from every part of the building. Blessedly, I had found my ear plugs (the best advice I had been given before leaving home) and was able to sleep most nights. On one occasion much later in Galicia, though, a man's snoring kept an entire *refugio* awake—earplugs or no—and he was sneered at for days after. Everyone knew him as "The Man Who Sawed Wood at Night," and anyone who had experienced the clamor he made avoided staying in the same *refugio* with him ever again.

My routine of dressing in clean clothes after showering at the end of the day and then sleeping in the same clothes was a wonderful way to get off early with a minimum of preparation. I was a rumpled mess, of course, but most other pilgrims followed the same dress code, so wrinkled clothes were of little interest to anyone. When I woke, usually because people started stirring in the darkness of the room and flash lights went on, I joined the line to use the toilet, brushed my teeth, pulled my hair up and out of the way with a tie, and went about stuffing my sleeping bag into its sack. With the constant readjustment of the contents of my backpack, it was my first chore each day to fit the box with Grace's ashes and then my sleeping bag back into place at the bottom before stuffing in everything else.

The Architect and I hadn't made a plan as to where we'd meet in the morning. I expected to see him somewhere near the espresso machine where several others had gathered in the soft morning light. I put my one euro coin into the machine and watched the thick black stream fill the small plastic cup that dropped into position. There were some options to add *leché* and *azúcar* which I didn't notice before the cup filled so I was left to sip on the strong, thick liquid plain, without the *leché* I would have preferred. The bitter taste was at least hot and I shrugged as I thought of the big cup of my favorite frothy *café con leché* I'd have when the bars opened in a couple of hours.

The now-stale bread from last night was chewy, but still delicious with my coffee. I ate standing next to the counter in the kitchen, expecting to see The Architect appear. People were coming in and out. Some retrieved food left overnight in the refrigerator and others prepared a breakfast of cereal or sweets and coffee and then left with a wave and a *"Buen Camino!"* I walked around the *refugio*, upstairs and down, looking for my friend, and calling out *"Hola! Hola!"* and *"Dove siete?"* (Where are you?) in Italian and then in English.

It seemed everyone was gone. Finally, I realized that The Architect must have left too. Taking a deep breath, I hoisted up my backpack, made the usual adjustments to the straps, put on my now-battered straw hat, and sun glasses and went out the door by myself. Disappointed that he hadn't waited for me, I fought off tears as I realized how much I enjoyed his company and was counting on his being with me for a couple of days longer. Some pilgrims who had stopped at the church in the village before setting out, now approached me looking curious. "Where's The Architect?" they asked "Isn't he walking with you today?" Many had seen us together the day before so they assumed we were making the walk together.

"No," I said. "I think he's gone off with some other friends earlier. Maybe I slept too long or took too much time getting ready. Hopefully I'll catch-up with him later on." I almost said, "If you see him, tell him I'm looking for him and to wait for me," but I thought better of it. Maybe he just wanted to move on and meet some other people. I would have to re-acquaint myself with my solitude.

The silhouette of my father's head and shoulders were visible over the driver's seat in front of me as I sat on the rough wool seat behind him. He wore a fedora and, as was his custom, a dark blue overcoat that made him look even more distinguished with his graying temples and mustache. We drove silently for what seemed like hours. I couldn't see out of the window next to me and I didn't know where we were going. The sweet smell of the pipe he smoked was familiar and reassuring. I clutched my brother's hand as he sat next to me looking sullen and expressionless. We had been separated and I wanted to be sure not to lose him again.

Later Grace would explain that the "school" where Frank and I had lived hadn't fed me and that's why I was sick and had to take my medicine. The malnutrition I had was more likely caused by loneliness, as much as neglect. Many years later I learned that the school was in fact a home for children—orphans and wards of the state of Rhode Island. I don't have any conscious memories of the place itself and I never got a reasonable, or even consistent, explanation as to why my brother and I were there. There was always a palpable feeling of shame when I brought up the subject and once again got an evasive answer. After a while I determined never to question her about it again.

I do remember being frightened—a deep threatening fear. Nothing was familiar. No one to ask. It was a feeling of being completely lost—a feeling I can still recall vividly. I occupied all my time in looking for my brother. Frank remembers images of a very large building but, very little else. We were very young, certainly before we were school age. The move to the farm was supposed to bring back my health and have Frank and I living together again—which it did, on both accounts.

Standing on the old wooden porch that ran the full length of the pale yellow Victorian farmhouse, I watched as my father backed the large black car out of the dirt drive and on to the single lane road that passed in front. The sound of crunching stones under the tires was loud and sharp. He almost hit the hand-painted "EGGS" sign as he maneuvered his way slowly out and quickly away. My brother stood next to me, staring after the car. I waved to it before turning and following Frank through the creaking door and back into the house. My father must have forgotten to kiss me good-bye.

CARRYING GRACE TO SANTIAGO

Walking out of Puente la Reina on the *Ruã de los Romeus*, I stopped to look at the Romanesque doorway of the Church of Santiago. The heavy wooden door was decorated with metal studs and framed by several ever-diminishing concentric stone columns and worn Moorish carvings. Even with some of the images worn away, the beauty of the door was compelling. I hesitated to take time to go in and see the interior, knowing I wanted to make it to Estella that day. As with so many other sites, I made a mental note to see it again some day as I continued across the famous bridge and out of town.

The early morning air was fresh and the sky clear. I turned onto a moist dirt path that crossed through fields sprouting with new green growth. The cotton sweatshirt I was wearing wasn't needed for long. The sun was already warm and it had risen only an hour before. My water supply was with The Architect so my first stop would be to buy some more water. I decided to get just two small bottles this time—when I found a market that was open—hoping to refill them later on if I came across a fountain safe for drinking.

I had walked less than a mile out when I arrived at a life-size contemporary sculpture of a pilgrim that marks the meeting of the two Caminos. Some pilgrims had left stones, a ribbon, a shell and a few wilted wildflowers there. People seemed to like to mark an intersection or a point of passage like this with a ceremonial token; maybe to signify their participation in the traditions of the ancient walk or just to mark the end of a stage or turning point. Others wedged notes into any available crevice or under a stone, with the hope that a friend, who might be passing later, would see them.

As I stood looking at the waymarker and the sculpture, trying to decipher the Spanish inscription, I heard in the distance, behind me, *"Señora, wait, señora!"* Again, looking back, I saw The Architect hurrying toward me, waving, as he had on the *Sierra del Perdón*. This time he was hobbling with the discomfort of his blisters. I stood smiling, waiting for my friend to catch-up.

"Hola, hola, señora! I say you to wait for me, my friend!" he said breathlessly. "I look for you everywhere! Maybe you not know I was in the toilet, hey?"

Forgetting those things which are behind,
and reaching forth unto those things which are
before, press toward the mark for the prize.

Paul's letter to the Phillipians 3:12-14

The Camino ambled on toward Estella through the furrowed, planted countryside. The Architect and I had reached a comfortable pace and we were making good time in the cool morning hours. Fields of different grains, grape vineyards, and acres of pruned cherry and apricot trees drew lines and patterns across the rolling hills, far into the distance. At times we walked next to streams still flowing with cool water from the Cantabrian Mountains we could see on the horizon.

A group of locals were gathering berries at the edge of a field by the side of the path. We stopped to talk with them and The Architect commented on their harvest. They said in a month's time the streambeds would be dry and the fields that weren't being cultivated would be brown and barren. The days were already very hot, and there were parched hillsides in evidence. We were fortunate to see the landscape still showing the green for which it was named—*Espagna Verde.*

The gatherers included a wizened old woman, bent and brown, who carried a cloth sack over her shoulder that hung to her knees. Two men and a young woman who made up the rest of the work party, all held plastic bags from shopping of a different sort. The tall man who first noticed us told The Architect they were there for their annual harvest of the wild berries—a kind of blueberry.

The harvesters walked with the quick steps of the guilty as they loaded their bags into the back of their new model car. The land apparently wasn't theirs and the men seemed hurried and uncomfortable with their gestures and explanations to The Architect. To make clear how long-standing their tradition of harvesting the berries had gone on, they explained that their aged grandmother, gesturing to the old woman busily picking, had been gathering those berries since she was a child. The matriarch looked up to flash a toothless smile.

Meadows of wildflowers—blue, yellow, pink—sprawled out beyond us where fields had been left to rest. In the hills there were small clusters of villages—some with what looked like ruined castles or churches perched on top. The ocher and russet stone mounds seemed to grow organically out of the earth of the same color. I wanted to capture some of the experience, the air, the smells, the sounds of chirping life by picking some flowers to dry in my journal but the flowers wilted in my sweaty hand before I could put them to rest.

The town of Cirauqui was just ahead of us and we began to look forward to finding a bar open where we could get a cup of coffee and maybe an omelette. At the very least, we might find somewhere comfortable and shady where we could sit and have some of the grapes, apples and cheese we were carrying from the night before.

The Basque word, "*Cirauqui*," means "nest of vipers." As we approached, I wondered if the name held a story about the temperament of the people who settled there and what kind of welcome we'd find. Some of the medieval walls that had once surrounded and protected the "vipers" are still in place and a labyrinth of twisting roads runs through the small village. Maybe it's the serpentine roads themselves that are the reason for the name.

The door of the church in Cirauqui, the *Iglesia San Román*, is a great example of 13th century church architecture from the period. It has the kind of Moorish influences in the arched and repeated lobes of the entrance that was becoming more common to see on that stretch of the Camino. I had read about the doorway just the night before in my "guidebook" pages and The Architect agreed it was worth stopping to see—but we would have to find coffee and something to eat first.

Following the small scallop shell markers painted on the houses along the street, we saw a man and woman in the road just ahead of us who were busily opening their bar and setting out signs that were meant to entice passersby. The man was carrying a small round metal table and a matching white chair and the woman, another chair. As he hurried back in through the door to bring out more seating, he glanced over his shoulder and called out *"Buenos dias!"* with a wave in our direction. The woman, who had arranged the table next to the building, offered us the place to sit down.

"Gracias, muchas gracias," we exclaimed. *"Buenos dias, señora!"* The Architect added with his warm and open smile. As we lowered our backpacks to the stones that formed the terrace area outside the bar, we ordered coffee, a *bocadillo* of local cheese and an omelette. I was soon sipping on my favorite *café con leché* and biting into a *bocadillo* of crusty bread filled with cheese and tomatoes. The Architect had ordered a *tortilla españole*, the potato omelette—he had his with the more customary ham included. In his usual way of enjoying everything so fully, he lavished praise on it and the chef.

"This is the best omelette ever cooked, *señora!* You take some. Take! Take!" he insisted, pushing his dish towards me.

"No, no, I'd love to. Thanks very much. *Muchas gracias,* but you know I'm a vegetarian—well, I mean, I don't eat meat."

"Oh, *si, si,* I remember this. Too bad for you, this time, I think."

After breakfast, we bought an extra bottle of water from the couple and once again, lifted our packs up and onto our backs. The couple came outside to say good-bye and wish us well. They waved as we walked on. *"Buen Camino!"* they both called out, and the ever-encouraging *"Ultreya!"*—"Go beyond!"

We walked through the quiet streets in the direction the bar owner had told us to go, looking for the *Iglesia San Roman* and its famous portal. Turning where he had said we'd find it, the old stone church stood just ahead of us.

The door was certainly worthy of its reputation. There were many bands of decorative figures and designs carved in the stone that surrounded the door itself. The concentric rhythms and delicate carvings were still clearly defined. There were some worn figures of saints and worshippers carved in the piers that seemed to support the arch and also over the door in the tympanum. I was glad to see how well the vipers had taken care of the door. We agreed that there wasn't enough time to go inside the church, if we were to stay on schedule and reach Estella that afternoon. The Architect crossed himself and muttered some words as we turned away to walk on.

After getting back on the path to the left of the plaza near the church, we followed it down a slope and out of town. Our delicious breakfast had left us relaxed and satisfied and we smiled at each other as we walked on with renewed contentment and a sense of purpose. We chatted and strolled along over rolling terrain for a short while until ahead of us we could see rows of cypress trees that appeared to line the path.

"*Dios, mi,* it is here we arrive on the *calzada romana!*" The Architect said.

We had come to the long stretch of Roman road, paved with rounded, dark stones 2,000 years ago, and distinguished by the tall cypress trees that lined it on either side. The Architect, in his usual joyous way, shared my sense of awe at walking where the early Romans had trod. In unison, we began to march on the stones as if we were among the legendary ranks of Roman foot soldiers marching to Santiago and then collapsed into laughter at our similar response to this ancient place.

The path rounded a hill and we descended slowly to a culvert that had the remains of a stone wall crossing it. Some large, dirt-covered rounded stones provided a way of crossing the culvert. They were once connected to another wall at the left, which was no longer standing. We saw several pilgrims around the ruin, taking pictures of the ancient stones and of each other.

"*Oh, dios, dios,* this is all that is of the famous Roman bridge. *Um-um-um,*" The Architect lamented, shaking his head. He'd read that the bridge was being restored by the architectural historical entity of Spain, but obviously, no work had begun. Judging from the activity around it, this bridge was a landmark that many walkers looked forward to reaching.

While I lowered my backpack to the ground with the help of the wall of the bridge behind me, The Architect scrambled down the side of the small hill to look more closely at the bridge construction. He said he thought the river below had always been just a small creek as it was now, judging from the span of the bridge. It was his guess that the Romans needed the bridge to cross the culvert with their carts and chariots more than for their foot soldiers.

The bridge and the stretch of Roman road before it are offered as historical proof that the Way of St. James actually followed a much earlier, already established road to Santiago long before the Christians laid claim to it. Some scholars believe that the *Via Lactea*, the stars that make up the Milky Way, led early man to the western regions of Iberia and on to the Atlantic coast to Finesterre (*finis terra*—the end of the earth) by pointing the way across what is now the Camino de Santiago. Two pilgrims in Pamplona told me they planned to walk at night when the skies were clear so that they could test the Milky Way directional theory.

There are several 5,000-year-old Neolithic dolmens on the Camino, evidence that the path was more ancient than just the time of the Romans. Some believe the Camino follows a strong magnetic energy line, a telluric current, across Spain to Santiago and it is that "pull" that holds the power that drew pilgrims along the path for so many centuries. The energy-line believers, say it's because of that current that walking the Camino has the ability to spiritually transform a pilgrim.

A few miles beyond the Roman bridge, we came to the *Rio Salado*. The Architect, who was always well-versed in the legends of the Camino, told me about a medieval tale of a group of pilgrims who were met by a couple of Navarese men who stood on the other side of the river. When the pilgrims asked if the water was safe to drink, they were told that it was and so they let their horses drink after the many dusty miles they had covered. In a few minutes, all of the horses were dead. The Navarese wanted the horses' skins—for what purpose, The Architect didn't know—and they devised this simple way to acquire as many skins as they needed. Obviously, rumor didn't travel along the path then as it does now. With pilgrims being forewarned of dangers ahead, as they are today, the river would not have claimed many horses.

The sun was high in the sky. We had been walking for a few hours and we were both getting hungry again. There was a shadeless field next to the path where we decided to stop to eat the remainder of our food from the night before. I unbuckled the belt from my pack and lifted it down and on to the dusty earth, happy to get some air on my back. I took off my hat to swipe at my brow with my sleeve.

Our supply of water was dwindling. The day grew hotter and the path dustier. Except for some shrubby bushes next to the path, there was no place to lie down out of the midday sun. When we walked through the silent villages along the way, we found that our timing was off. Aside from our stop in Cirauque, there were no markets open to buy food or water and no bars to get a drink or something to eat.

In the early afternoon, we entered a seemingly deserted, shuttered village and took solace in finding a large rectangular stone basin that was bubbling up and filled with cool water. A bare pipe was set in the middle and spouted a stream of water a foot or so skyward in a meek effort to suggest a "fountain." We took off our boots and socks and lowered our sore and swollen feet into the pool that formed next to the central cascade. The fountain was originally little more than a trough for cows being driven through the square to the pastures beyond, but now however, the paved, treeless square where the fountain stood was a gathering place for the villagers on cooler days or evenings and the fountain was its focus.

The stone and stucco buildings surrounding the square shimmered with the heat. I squinted out from behind my sunglasses and raised an arm for added shade as I looked around the square. A slight breeze swept up dusty puffs at one side of the plaza. One or two of the small buildings had a shrub or tree next to the doorway. There were neither flowers planted nor any flower boxes. The sharp and rapid barking of a dog chained to the side of a building nearby was the only evidence of life.

The sun was painfully hot on my skin and I marveled that The Architect could walk without a hat. He untied a sort of bandanna he had around his neck, soaked it in the cool water and draped it over his head to cool himself. I scooped my porous straw hat down into the pool of water and quickly dumped what water it would hold onto my head. We both laughed as the water ran down and soaked our hair, our faces and our clothes. I wondered if the village people would be offended that we were sitting with our feet in their fountain but The Architect insisted that people love the pilgrims and besides, "The cows would drink here in old days, why not we take comfort?"

A wooden cow trough stood outside the barn on the Parker's farm. When I stood next to it, I was just the same height as the cows as they lowered their heads to lap the water. I must have been three or four years old the day my father backed out of the driveway and left my brother and me at the farm. Even though I didn't know why we were left there, our life on the farm was to be at the center of my happiest childhood memories.

The Parkers took in foster children and, since they had no children of their own and needed help on the farm, it seemed a good choice for them. There were two other children there—wards of the state of Rhode Island—the twins, Frankie and Freddie, who were a few years older than my brother. They were there because their mother had been "put away." I remember not being sure what that meant but the boys didn't want to talk about it. I imagined their mother was behind bars somewhere with wild eyes and disheveled hair. The twin's father was never mentioned but they had an older sister who came to visit them occasionally. She was always in a hurry and angry. She didn't speak to me, except to say "Hi, Sis." "Sissy" was the name the Parkers and the boys gave me. It was what Frank called me when I was born—his little sister. My brother was just, "Brother," in some illogical attempt to avoid confusion between the two Franks.

"Aunt Alice" Parker was tall and always wore her hair in braids that wrapped over the front of her head and were pinned at the back. Her cotton dresses had small, all-over patterns and, on cool mornings, she'd wear a maroon sweater with big buttons up the front and pockets on both sides. The pockets bulged with something—either hankies, large black keys, or a pencil and note pad used to "jot" notes to herself and lists—always lists. "Just a minute, Sissy, gotta' do some jottin'," she'd say as she paused in the midst of a task. It was impossible to see her skin through her thick stockings. Her everyday brown shoes were scruffy, sturdy, and laced up the front with a thick heel that added to her height. Her Sunday shoes were very much the same, except that they were black and shiny.

Aunt Alice struck a large iron bell that was set up on the porch to call Mr. Parker and the boys in for lunch, and again for dinner. He'd arrive at the midday meal and at the dinner table wearing overalls and a plain shirt, heavy dark boots and carrying a rumpled hat—his face browned and scored by the sun. Before he came to the table, I could hear him at the water pump outside the kitchen door. He'd prop his hat on a nearby bush, then wash his hands and wipe his face and neck with a cloth that hung on the pump. After he said grace, he said very little else as we sat around the large kitchen table. If any of us children didn't want to eat something that was on our plate, however, his soft voice just stated the rules and we were kept in our seats until we finished.

The only time Mr. Parker included me in anything the boys were doing was when he took the tractor out to pull the hay wagon in the fields across the road. The boys would gather up the mounds of hay into the wagon and I could ride along. I remember the smell of the warm hay and my joy at rolling in the soft piles of the fragrant grasses as the boys tossed clumps with their pitchforks at the slow moving wagon. I was showered with hay from all sides —left, right and center. When the wagon was filled to over-flowing, we all rode back to the barn perched high on the top of the hay mound while Mr. Parker slowly coaxed the old tractor across the fields. I saw him smile one day as we turned into the barn.

Walking through the farms and vineyards of northern Spain heightened my memories of life on the farm in Rhode Island. This part of Spain is the very opposite of the arid lands in the south, and, except for the climate, seemed to me in every other way to be very much like the Parker's farm. The sounds and the smells of the farms: the fresh fields of grass; the pungent smell of manure; the chickens clucking and roosters crowing; the cows and sheep nibbling away their day; people moving slowly about their chores brought it all back to me.

While the boys were away for the morning with Mr. Parker in the fields, Aunt Alice gave me chores too. She had a small basket for me to carry and she took me with her to gather eggs in the hen house. The thrill of finding a warm egg under a hen as I reached my small hand beneath her was like going on an Easter morning egg hunt everyday. Placing the two or three eggs I usually found into the basket I carried, I felt the thrill of being the bearer of something really important, a treasure for all to share. When I'd spread chicken feed in their pen and watch the chickens' bobbing heads as they pecked at their meal, I felt I was saying "thank you" to them for their bounty—a fair exchange.

After milking the few cows they kept, and letting the cream rise in the covered buckets resting in the pantry, Aunt Alice churned butter from the fresh cream. She stood over a column-like wooden device, raising and lowering a wooden pole centered inside it. I watched as she stirred and mixed, canned and baked on the old wood stove in the large kitchen. The gleaming glass mason jars sat, steam still rising from their "sanitizin'," all lined-up on the oil-cloth covered table top in the center of the room. The jars in turn would be filled with the stewed tomatoes, green beans, corn, peas, squash, succotash, blackberry and blueberry jams and boiled and pickled beets that would feed us over the months ahead. We ate everything from the farm. Buying groceries at a store was only an occasional event for the Parkers.

Aunt Alice was a genius at making vegetables taste delicious and at creating desserts from the berries the boys and I gathered in the woods on our afternoon adventures. While I knelt on one of the painted wooden chairs, I was sometimes given the job of sifting flour or stirring batter for strawberry short cake, blueberry buckle, and my favorite, blueberry roly-poly, a moist cake that was steamed in a covered pot over boiling water on top of the wood stove and served with lemon sauce. The fragrance of breads and muffins baking, and fresh pies and cakes cooling on a shelf in the pantry are among my most treasured memories of the times my brother and I spent on the farm.

Every summer day was closed with the ceremony of the four of us children gathered all in a line on the dirt path next to the back porch. Our enameled wash basins rested in front of us—chest high for me—on the porch floor. Standing above us on the porch, Aunt Alice poured hot water from a large blue kettle into each of our basins and we washed with a shared bar of Ivory soap and our own rough cloths. The boys and I would then see who could throw the soapy water from our basins farthest onto the grass behind us. I never won.

Aunt Alice never showed me any affection, nor held and consoled me when I was sick or crying because the boys had teased me. I don't remember her reading me a story or showing any pleasure in my behavior. But the calm and dependable routine of our life on the farm was very reassuring. Knowing what was expected, when we got up in the morning, what the chores were, when we went to bed, was a blessing. Without Grace's frequent explosions and my constant anxiety that I'd say or do something to upset her, life on the farm was a wonderful respite.

Both my brother and I thrived. I don't remember questioning why we were there and neither of us wanted to leave. There were to be many other periods when Frank and I would spend time away with Grace's relatives in New York City or back on the farm with the Parkers for a visit. It was her nerves, we were told. She needed a rest.

A new moon teaches gradualness and
deliberation and how one gives birth
to oneself slowly. Patience with small
details makes perfect a large work.

Rumi

Our pace was slowing and we made more frequent stops to deal with our blisters and for me to rest from the weight of my backpack. I knew The Architect was very uncomfortable even though he didn't complain. The moleskin plasters were not giving him much relief. His blisters had broken and were bleeding. With our feet swelling in the heat, we could expect still more blisters and, when I checked, it looked likely that I'd lose another toenail.

The rest of the afternoon is very vague in my memories of that day. Only hazy images come to mind: the shimmering heat waves rising in front of us, the dusty earth clouding around our feet, crows cawing and diving in the fields at our left and right. I was very hungry. My strength was fading and I wondered if I was going to make it to Estella. Every step was painful and my shoulders ached from the weight of my pack. My back was wet with sweat where the pack pushed in on me and my sunglasses kept sliding down my nose with the sweat dripping from my forehead. The glasses, with their fashionable small round lenses were next to useless in the penetrating sun. I vowed to look for some others when I reached a town where I could find a store that sold them.

Throughout the remaining hours that we walked that afternoon, we spoke very little. I felt comfortable walking silently with The

Architect. We only needed to look at each other and gesture to know what the other was thinking. Since leaving the side of a small creek where we soaked our feet, and I took time to do some drawings, we had passed no other pilgrims. The extraordinary heat of the day had obviously driven most people inside. Other pilgrims from Puente la Reina had probably planned better than we had and set out for Estella much earlier. They were also most likely showered and taking their *siesta* while we still trudged along. The thought of being clean and cool, and lying in a bed in a quiet room became my focus.

The Architect was always good-natured and even though he was hobbling with his painful feet, he humored me. "Come, *señora*, we make funny pilgrims! We must walk straight and not, how you say? Like this," and he shuffled like a bent old man, leaning on a make-believe cane.

"See, this is the way we must walk." Straightening his shoulders, he limped along for a few steps and realized his style didn't look very much better. He fell into gales of laughter and I, once again, realized how grateful I was to have him there with me. Had I been walking alone with Grace, my afternoon might have been filled with defeat.

Grace couldn't see any possibility for success in anyone's endeavor and if they happened to succeed, her negativity said it was probably "fixed" or "they had a connection." There was usually a raised eyebrow and a wistful look on her face when I suggested I'd like to do something wonderful, if possibly difficult. "Well, go ahead and try but don't be disappointed if you don't make it." Or, more often, "Hmmmph. You think you're so smart? See what a fool you'll make of yourself. Who do you think you are, anyway?" as she slumped back into her sadness or drew herself out of her sedentary roost to go to the kitchen to get something to eat.

Eating had become solace for her recurring depression and as she aged, her girth was evidence of it. She had also found comfort in cooking the fragrant, rich meals of her childhood, spent between two cultures: that of her immigrant Italian parents and her desire to be *"un' Americana."* A large pot of tomato sauce would simmer on the stove in our kitchen on an average weekend afternoon. The fragrance of garlic and onions sautéing, of sausage and meatballs sizzling filled the air. Broccoli or cauliflower were steamed and resting in bowls on the kitchen table, ready to be breaded and fried.

She would occasionally let me help her with dipping the vegetables in frothy whisked eggs and then into salted flour on a plate, back into the egg mixture and finally into breadcrumbs on still another plate. The vegetables waited in turn on kitchen towels as each batch was fried and then returned to the towels to drain. Grace was comfortable in the role of cook. It was safe; she understood its width and breadth and felt her own authority in it.

She taught me to assemble lasagna with plenty of the three cheeses that make up the dish—parmigiana, mozzarella and ricotta, adding a whipped egg to the ricotta to make it more spreadable; adding to the flavor of the sauce with a cup of espresso as it simmered in the last hour. She stuffed and rolled flank steak with sautéed onions, pieces of bread that had been dried in the oven, crumbled sausage, oregano, basil, fresh ground black pepper, and an egg to make *braciola*. Red peppers were skinned after charring in a brown paper bag in the oven and then cut into strips and put into jars to marinate with olive oil, chunks of garlic and sprigs of basil. She was at her softest when she was cooking and even though she could be impatient with my mistakes, I enjoyed learning to cook with her. I wondered if I had ever told her so.

We walked alongside a large olive grove and crossed an ancient bridge and then, as if by magic, we were in Estella. I had been following The Architect who walked several feet in front of me for the last hour, always looking back to see that I was still there and nodding to me, saying, "Just a little more, *señora*, a little more. *Brava, señora, brava.*"

It was late in the day, certainly past five o'clock, and it was doubtful that there would be any beds available at the *refugio*. Just the thought that we'd be able to stop walking and lie down on something, even the floor, was enough to get me through the door and standing at the table in front of the supervisor of the building, ready to show my Pilgrim's Passport and pay the requisite euros for shelter.

Each *refugio* had its own culture, which was often determined by the person in charge of running the place. Some were very casually run—you simply entered, signed a book, stamped your own Pilgrim's Passport and your money was collected when the overseer had the opportunity to drop by. When you entered other *refugio*s, however, you had an instant sense of the authority of the person in charge.

Such was the case in Estella. Each bed is specifically assigned—no self-determination here! After paying the fee and signing-in, the manager introduced himself with an air of pride in being the host of the building. He gave me and The Architect our bed assignments, which were a shared bunk, he wrote down the bed number next to our names and recited the rules of the house in part English and part Spanish, with an occasional French, *"comprenez-vous?"* There seemed to be so many regulations. I couldn't understand very much of what he was saying. The Architect kept repeating *"si, si,"* as he helped me out of my backpack. In Spanish he tried to explain to the man that I needed to lie down.

Our bed, as it happened, was right next to one of the two bathrooms each of which had two showers. They had seen heavy use that afternoon and there was a lot of water on the floors and one of the toilets was stopped-up. The Architect gestured to me to take the lower bunk of our bed assignment and we both took off our boots

and stood in line for a shower. By the time it was my turn, there was no warm water but it didn't matter. I stood on my dirty clothes while I showered and gave them a brief rinse on the floor before turning off the shower and getting dressed in the clean clothes I had retrieved from my backpack.

All of the more than sixty beds available were taken by the time we showered. It was crowded inside the sleeping rooms where it smelled musky, or worse, from the non-functioning toilet. The small enclosed outdoor space behind the building was also filled with people sitting on the ground, or on make-shift seats fashioned from over-turned planters. They were talking, sharing a bottle of wine or writing in their journals. I walked out to find a place to hang my clothes before lying down to rest. I had decided not to go with The Architect to shop for food, even though I was very hungry and had nothing to eat for the next day as well. I knew my strength would not hold out and I longed to rest my throbbing head.

I was standing with my hands full of my wet and dripping clothes, looking for a place to hang them, when I heard a familiar voice.

"Hello! Hey, hello! American Woman!" Turning, I saw a bicycle, with an attached trailer behind it, resting against the garden wall and Demetri sitting on the ground next to it. He jumped up from the group he was talking with to come over to embrace me.

"*Phew! Mon Dieu!* You are *fatigué*—tired, no? How far did you walk today?" he asked.

"Oh, not far. Just from Puente la Reina, about 20 kilometers (12 miles). But, yes, I'm really tired. I feel kinda' shaky, too. I walked with a friend, The Architect, you know him? Well, he thinks we should have had more sugar and salt and water too, of course."

While I hung my clothes over some wires meant to trail flowers along the wall surrounding the outdoor area, Demetri and I shared our stories of the days since we had last seen each other in the Pyrenees at Zubiri. I asked him why he hadn't gotten any further than Estella. Riding his bicycle, I thought he'd have reached León or at least Burgos by then.

"Oh, *oui*, well . . . you see . . . I met a girl on the way, near to Pamplona. A Dutch girl. *Tre jolie!* You know, *la femme*, heh? She was biking and camping also. So we thought to see some of the environs there and rest for the day or two. *Baa! Quel dommage!* It did not work! I mean, me and the Dutch girl." He circled his finger in the air around the side of his head, "She was, how you say? . . . nuts! " He shrugged his shoulders and added, "*C'est la vie!*"

I told him I had been walking with The Architect since just after the *Sierra del Perdón* and that we had been making pretty good time. While I was talking, my body began to shake and I thought I was going to lose my balance. Reaching for something to steady myself, Demetri looked alarmed and grabbed my hand to lead me back to my bunk. Then he rushed away to get some water. My head ached so much that I didn't dare move it and I was very hot all over. I began to have chills and sweat at the same time. Demetri knelt and hurriedly handed me a cup of water as I sat on the edge of my bunk.

"Where is The Architect? I will find him." he said as he began to stand and leave.

"No, no. It's okay. He went to see the cathedral—to the Pilgrim's Blessing. He'll be back later on. I'll be okay. I just need to sleep," I explained, as I handed him back his cup. I put my pounding head down and soon fell into a deep and delirious sleep.

As I woke from time to time, I was aware of two or three pilgrims gathered around my bunk and I could hear each one with a theory as to what was wrong with me and how to remedy it. Should they call a doctor? Was there a doctor in the *refugio*? The faces came and went. Someone brought a piece of fruit. I fell in and out of delirium—time went by. It was very dark and quiet when I woke again. The Architect was smiling at me. He was stroking my forehead and calling me softly as if from a great distance.

"*Señora, señora.*" He knelt next to my bed and held my head up as he tried to have me sip some orange juice. "Drink, drink, *señora*. You need this. It is for the sugar." He brought me something to eat, too—I don't remember what it was—but my nausea wouldn't let me swallow it.

"In the night, if you need me . . . here," he implored softly. "Maybe you need me, you touch the bed like this." He showed me a short-handled broom that was lying nearby and demonstrated how I could poke his mattress above me to wake him up. Then he dug into his backpack that was resting on the floor next to our bunkbed. He took out a clean sock and wet it with cold water from the sink in the bathroom next to us and laid the damp, cool sock on my forehead then poured me a cup of water from a new supply he had gotten at the market.

"I will sleep now. I must go very, very early. Only two days more for me. Then, I must work again. I go and you rest here for some days, maybe two."

"Yes, I know, you have to keep going. I understand. Thank you for everything. *Muchas gracias.*" Then I added, "I'll be looking for your buildings in Spain." I spoke in a whisper. The Architect bent closer to me.

Struggling to smile and look encouraging, I said, "You know, I don't even know your name. My name's 'Maureen.'"

"*Maur-e-e-een,*" He sounded out slowly. "Yes, this is nice name. Pretty name, like you, *señora*. Pretty woman in here, too." he said as he touched his chest. His soft voice sounded gruff as he whispered.

"I am Oracio—'Horace' in English, no? He was Egyptian guide and protector to kings. I made good protector to you and Grace, no, *señora*?" he asked.

He bent down still closer and we kissed on both cheeks. "You will be okay now, Maureen. *A dios, amiga. Buen Camino,* hey?"

Today, like every other day, we wake up empty
and frightened. Don't open the door to the study
and begin reading. Take down a musical instrument.
Let the beauty we love be what we do.
There are hundreds of ways to kneel and
    kiss the ground.

Rumi

As I was waking up, I could just make out the sound of someone quietly sweeping the floor of the room overhead. My watch said quarter to eight. I rubbed my eyes, swung my feet out of the bunk, and sat up. Looking around the room that had been so crowded the night before, I saw that there was no one else there.

The host of the hostel would soon be coming to let me know that I had over-stayed my welcome. Pilgrims are expected to leave most *refugios* by about eight in the morning. If you needed to rest, you could stay for an extra day or possibly two in exchange for work. Some people clean the bathrooms or sweep the floors, mop the kitchen (if there is one) or pick up the grounds. The facilities had to be made ready by early afternoon when the next group of pilgrims would begin to arrive. I gathered up my soap and toothbrush, along with my towel and decided I'd have a few minutes to consider doing that or just walking on.

When I got back to my bunk from the toilet, I thought I felt well enough to continue, at least as far as Los Argos—about eight miles ahead. If I felt strong enough when I got there, I could try to go further. My ersatz-guide showed that after Los Argos, the next town that had services and a *refugio* was Torres del Rio. That was eighteen miles from where I stood. Unless there was a town somewhere between Los Argos and Torres del Rio where I could find a *refugio*, I'd probably just stop in Los Argos that day. It was tantalizing to think that I might be able to catch-up with The Architect later on or maybe the following day.

Moving very slowly, I sat on the edge of my bunk and replaced the comfortable flip-flops I had been wearing with clean sox and my dusty boots. The damp, semi-clean clothes I had retrieved from the line in the back garden would have to dry hanging outside my back-pack for a couple of hours. I laced up my boots and rearranged the plastic box with Grace in it, my sleeping bag duffel, clothes and toiletries in the pack then hoisted it up and stood wobbling for a minute as I got my balance. After securing the belt at my waist, I bent down to pick up the bread and fruit that had been left by my bed dur-ing the night and tucked the bounty into a side pocket of the pack. I took a long drink of juice from the bottle The Architect had left for me, and set off out the door and onto the streets of Estella. *Andiamo, Grace!*

The old part of town has ancient beginnings and, therefore, narrow winding streets. It was originally a Roman outpost which King Sancho Ramirez is given credit for rebuilding in 1090. Later on, kings of Navarra used it as a residence during the Middle Ages and it was a pivotal resting and regrouping point on the pilgrims' way to Santiago. Today there are many old palaces, mansions and towers that are evidence of its having once been a very prosperous town.

The air was fresh and cool when I left the *refugio* and wandered up the cobbled street following the Camino markers. Along the way, I stopped at a bar where some other pilgrims were having breakfast and ordered my usual *café con leché*, an omelette with cheese, and a soft sweet roll. The meal gave me new energy. I realized I hadn't eaten since the afternoon before—even the dry roll was delicious.

I had planned to visit the churches and the local museum but the others at the bar told me the museum wouldn't be open for a half hour and visiting it and the churches would take a couple of hours. I decided it would be wiser to do most of the day's walking in the relatively cool morning hours and just give myself a quick walking tour of Estella's highlights.

Turning back towards the *refugio*, I saw the steep flight of stone steps that go directly to the door of the 12th century fortified church of *San Pedro de la Rúa*. The church with its tower is a prominent landmark of Estella and you can easily see the tower from all over the city.

The main doorway and surrounding portal of the massive building have the beautifully carved, lobed and multi-arched Moorish decorations that are so common in Navarra. Here again was a breathtaking example. I was disappointed not to be able to get inside the church to see the column of three entwined snakes I had read about. The doors were closed and locked. There's evidently a 13th century relic of St. Andrew in a silver shrine and a supposedly a beautiful, damaged, cloister there as well.

Having no option, I retraced my steps down the broad flight of stairs and, with directions from one of the pilgrims I met at breakfast, I found the *Palacio de los Reyes de Navarra*, the palace of the kings of Navarra. Also built in the 12th century, this huge building is a rare example of Romanesque civil architecture; most sizeable buildings of the time were built for the church. Part of the building now houses a museum entirely devoted to a little-known painter, engraver and writer, Gustavo de Maetzu, who lived from 1887 until 1947 and spent most of those years in Estella. The museum collection is comprised entirely of donations made by his family and heirs.

On the front of the palace are two columns on either side of the main entrance, which bracket a series of archways. The capitals of the columns have deep stylized carvings. One shows Roland fighting the Moor, Ferragut, both sitting astride horses with swords drawn. The horses look impossibly posed there, balanced on a ring that encircles the column. On the other column, there are strange creatures challenging animals playing musical instruments. I was happy to see these quarrelsome groups and smiled as I turned to find the last building I had wanted to see in Estella, the church of *San Miguel Arcángel*.

San Miguel is situated in the *Mercado Viejo*—the old market place— and the exterior of the building itself is very plain. The style is somewhere between Romanesque and Gothic but the church is known mostly, again, for its exquisite doorway. Considered to be one of Navarra's finest examples of Romanesque sculpture, I thought it was one of the prettiest and most elaborately carved I had seen so far.

The repeated concentric arches that led the eye ever deeper and deeper into the entrance way—the door itself—were carved with saints blessing, musicians playing, people embracing, children praying, animals feeding, angels flying, men and women working in the earth, mothers with babies, people on horseback, warriors with swords drawn and, as always, the ever present threatening monsters and ghouls surrounding them all and tormenting sinners in Hell. In the center, in the tympanum—the space over the door God, or maybe it was meant to be Jesus, sat in peace amongst the saints and angels. The life described in those carvings, done so many centuries before, could easily be a description of life today. People busy living life, threatened by all sorts of imagined demons—finding peace in the unknown.

Following the markers once again, I headed out through a newer more open area west of Estella, and saw the "Woman from Berlin" ahead of me on the path. She and her husband walked separately. I never saw them together on the path but in the evenings at the *refugios* they would share a bunk. They usually had a drink or a meal together at a bar at the end of a day's walk. She was the one talking. He would nod and seemed to be listening to her but he didn't offer much to the conversation.

We said "hello" at a crossroads where the signs offered two ways: one, the traditional Camino path and the other a detour pointing in the direction of the Bodegas Irache Winery. The two large stone buildings that made up the winery complex were on a rise in the distance not far from where we stood. One of the pilgrims I met at breakfast told me the winery had mounted two separate spigots—one for water and one for wine—on the side of the former monastery building and the beverages were available just about all day long. I stood in front of the sign considering which way to go and said out loud "Well, I think I'll take the more direct path."

The Woman from Berlin had already turned and was walking in the direction of the winery. She called back over her shoulder to me, "I think I'll take the path with more fun!"

Yes, that's it! I thought. *Don't forget to have some fun, Maureen!* So I followed her in the direction of the wine. The worrier in me prodded,

But you'll never catch-up with The Architect at this rate! You got sick yesterday from god-knows-what, remember? You can't start the morning with red wine! RED wine! You get headaches from red wine!

Shh-h-h, another voice responded. *Everything's just fine. It's all working out perfectly.*

The Woman from Berlin continued walking ahead of me through the vast expanse of vineyards that ran all the way up to and around the first large stone building. That building looked like it was the bottling plant for the winery with trucks pulled up to loading platforms along one side. The 12th century monastery that sat further up on the rise of the hill just behind the bottling plant was where we'd find the well-known spigots. The monastery had been restored not long ago and was open to visitors during limited hours in warm weather.

When I arrived a few minutes behind The Woman from Berlin, she was laughing and pointing up to something above our heads opposite the wall with the spigots. Looking in the direction she was pointing, I saw a camera mounted high on a fence facing the building and focused on the spigots. The light on it was blinking. We were being recorded. There were two plaques on either side of the spigots. One read:

> Pilgrim, if you want to reach Santiago with
>
> strength and vitality, take a drink of this
>
> great wine and toast to happiness.

The other had a more practical tone:

> To drink without abuse
>
> we invite you with pleasure.
>
> To take the wine with you
>
> It will have to be bought.

The Woman from Berlin and I stood together drinking the wine from scavenged cups and mugging for the camera. We talked a little about our experiences on the Camino, as was the custom. She told me her name was Hanna and her husband was Horst. I smiled inwardly at the image of the two of them as a vaudeville act "*. . . and now presenting, that world famous dancing duo, Hanna and Horst!*"

PILGRIM IF YOU WANT TO REACH SANTIAGO WITH STRENGTH AND VITALITY TAKE A DRINK OF THIS GREAT WINE AND TOAST TO HAPPINESS

Pilgrim if you want to reach Santiago with strength and vitality, take a drink of this great wine and toast to happiness

Almost everyone walking the Camino is given a moniker, a name that distinguishes him or her. It's not something you can just decide to call yourself—it's the way other people refer to you in conversation and sometimes what identifies your purpose for walking. Hanna and Horst were known as "The Woman and Man from Berlin" most likely because that's all that anyone knew about them. Hanna told me I was known as "The American Woman Who is Carrying her Mother." Quite a mouthful. I often made-up names for the people I saw on the Camino. I wondered what I would have called me.

As we stood talking, I could see Hanna's husband in the distance beyond the acres of vineyards, walking back to re-join the Camino. He had already been there having his morning wine. He looked back and waved. We both returned the greeting.

This was the second time I had seen Hanna and Horst walking together. Horst had made three trips to Santiago already—two by himself and another one with Hanna and a friend of hers the year before. Hanna said she had thought she was going to learn patience and understanding and she would be a better person if she walked the Camino.

"But it wasn't to be-e-e-e!" she shook her bowed head and lamented. "I was very irritable with my friend! Always impatient with her and very mean. Nothing was going the way I expected it and I just blamed HER for everything that bothered me! Then I noticed everyone around me was annoying, too! They were all so stupid and silly. Well, it was a complete failure! *I* was a complete failure—and I disappointed myself," she went on to explain. "So, now, this year, I am walking alone and I will hopefully find a side of me that I think is there, *ya?*"

We finished our cups of wine and took time to top-off our water bottles with water from the spigot. Hanna wanted to carry some of the wine for later so she emptied a partially full water bottle she had in her waistband and refilled it with the wine, "something to go *mit* lunch, *ya?*"

Soon we were back on the spur trail that would take us to the Camino path. We saw Horst looking back toward us. He stood waiting for a while until we were within earshot of him and then he walked on. Horst didn't speak any English, although Hanna said, with a *"harrumph!"* he knew it very well. He refused to speak, she said, because that way, he could be more within himself.

"He wants people to think he can't speak English or French because then he can ignore people when he wants to! That's why he does it. Ya, Horst, am I right?" Horst? You see, he's just being difficult," Hanna decided.

Horst was simply quiet in any language. I don't remember him speaking much even in his native German without prodding—and further explanation—from Hanna. He had "dark moments," she explained and walking the Camino was an inexpensive way of taking some time to be outside with nature, doing physical activity, and still having the companionship of other pilgrims—when he wanted it.

"There are cheap flights to Greece for him but, when he's there on the beach, he's all alone. This is not good for him, you understand, ya? And, also, I don't like the beach."

Hanna was proud of her husband's experiences on the Camino. "He is authority on the history and traditions of the Camino, ya? What would you like to know about it? I will ask him," she said encouraging me to offer Horst a challenge.

"Horst!" she called ahead to him and then, in German, proceeded to ask him my question. I wanted to know what his favorite region or town was and why he liked it. Continuing to walk ten or more feet ahead of us, Horst would turn his head in response to Hanna's question, calling back a few seemingly disconnected words and she listened.

"*Ya, ya,*" she would call out in return to him, "*Was ist das, Horst?*"

"I don't think he's right about that. Yesterday he said he liked Galicia; now it is Navarra! He only does that to be difficult!" she shook her head and looked at him with a glowering stare. "*OUFF,* he is too much, *ya?*"

Since Horst had walked to Santiago in different seasons, he could advise pilgrims on what to expect in the spring, summer, or fall. His highest recommendation was that one could have the best experience in the late fall.

Through Hanna's interpreting, commentary and editorializing, Horst described, "Few pilgrims walk in the fall so the *refugios* are not crowded, the air is cool, also, ya? Sometimes it is very cold, brr-r-r-r," she emphasized, rubbing her forearms.

"If your time is good, and your plan is right, you can have harvesting of the grapes for yourself! The path is right through the vineyards in Rioja wine district. You will see! Just like here but more! Much more!"

"And," Hanna went on, "You can have nice HOT showers, and the restaurants aren't crowded either—he told me that before."

While Hanna was translating and editing Horst's comments, he began to recite a poem or some other rhythmic passage, to no one in particular, at full voice—loud and clear.

"*OUFF! Ach tu lieber!* What Horst? What? Oh, he's just being silly," Hanna decreed with a flip of her hand. "Horst! Stop it!" she called up to him as he picked up his pace and was no longer able to hear us. He waved over his shoulder and continued his recitation.

It was hard to imagine a less compatible couple than Hanna and Horst as pilgrims walking together on the Camino. They were so different in temperament and I shook my head at how they managed to make a life together.

I needed to have a break from Hanna's chatter so I decided it was time for me to make a personal stop behind a dense and broad bush next to the path. I said good-bye to her and cautiously walked off the trail. We agreed we'd probably see each other later in Los Argos, where we both planned to stop for the night. With experience, I learned that if I liked the relative cover of a near-by bush, usually many other pilgrims had liked it as well, so I was sure to place my feet carefully as I waved and said *"Buen Camino"* to Hanna.

Notice how each particle moves.
Notice how each person has just arrived here
    from a journey.
Notice how each wants a different food.
Notice how the stars vanish as the sun comes up,
    and how all streams stream toward the ocean.

Rumi

J ust as it seemed to be true of Hanna and Horst, my parents came from opposite sides of every measure of compatibility. When I was a teenager and thought about romantic love and how people "found" each other, I often wondered what had drawn them to each other. They hadn't always stayed together though. My father left Grace at least twice, that I remember. Yet, his devotion to her must have been genuine. Sorting through some of my mother's things when I moved her to a nursing home, I came across love letters he had written a few years before he died, pledging his love, devotion and his need for her. I don't think Grace would have returned his feelings—and yet she kept the letters.

In a photo I have of my father taken when he was about seven years old, he's sitting on a carved wooden high back Victorian chair. He told me it had a deep rose-colored velvet seat, part of a set that came from the dining room of their fourteen-room house. He was wearing small, round, wire-rimmed glasses and a formal tweed suit with knickers for trousers, long stockings and highly polished, laced-up shoes that rose above his ankles. There's no joy in his soft eyes.

He had two Shetland ponies as pets and was expected to learn to care for them and ride them properly. He admitted to me though that he never did either, leaving the task of the ponies' care to the man who did the gardening and drove his mother in one of their two early model automobiles. His lack of physical prowess was a constant annoyance to his father who wanted him to be more "manly," and physically strong. If wishing could make it so.

His family most likely had its American roots in the Irish immigration of the mid-1800s although, until he was in his late fifties when he saw some early family documents, he believed he was Welsh and English and that his ancestors had arrived in the 1700s. With the bigotry toward the Irish of Boston, my father's socially conscious mother no doubt wanted to protect their privileged life in Winchester, Massachusetts, from any association with the Irish poor streaming into New York and Boston at the time.

Born in Troy, New York in 1902, an only child, my father was a product of the Edwardian manners of the time and, probably more so, of his cold and controlling mother. He grew up in Winchester where his father was an industrialist who held a couple of patents; one on a process for manufacturing and stabilizing patent leather to withstand the heat of shipping it across the Equator. My father seldom spoke of his family, certainly nothing about his father, except to say that he had left the scene sometime long before my father had begun classes at Harvard. When he returned home shortly after his graduation in 1924, he found some of the staff packing the household and covering furniture. They explained that his mother had left on a long trip. He didn't see her again until many years later when they met for a brief visit and an attempt at reconciliation. It must not have gone well—I never met her.

At Harvard he attended classes with the Boston Brahmins—the Cabots and the Lodges, but didn't socialize with them, to his mother's dismay. He was considered to not have enough cachet, or the right family background. He joined the track team and excelled, breaking a Harvard record for the sprint, or the dash or was it the mile? He spent most of his time reading and writing poetry and short stories. He tutored other students in English and was mentored by some of the most respected professors teaching at Harvard at the time. I no longer remember the names he told me with such pride.

He was "bookish," slim in build, and not tall. He enjoyed dressing well and always carried himself with an air that belied the fact that he wasn't a particularly successful and certainly not a wealthy man. His childhood had been peppered with illnesses: several bouts with pneumonia, scarlet fever, measles, mumps and influenza during the terrible epidemic of 1918. Grace often said that sickness was probably his way of

getting his mother's attention. Grace could sometimes have remarkable insights. He continued the attention-getting technique through-out his life and died at the age of sixty-three shortly after his fourth heart attack.

Maria Grazia Carolina Caputo was born in a tenement on the lower east side of New York City in the sweltering heat of the summer of 1910. She arrived two years after her mother, paternal grandfather, and aunts came from Naples to join her father.

Francesco Caputo entered Ellis Island in 1906 at the height of the economic depression in Italy that followed the break-up of the monarchy. He was twenty-six years old when he arrived. He was a poet, a painter, a fabric designer, and an inventor. In his later years he would build a microscope, a radio, and a camera—grinding his own lenses and following his own designs. Grace's collection of his watercolors, mostly landscapes of Italy and the American south—some of which hang on the walls of the room where I sit now—were her most treasured legacy from him.

During the first years after his arrival in New York, Francesco lived in a room he shared with several other young men on Thompson Street on the lower East Side. He found work doing a variety of menial jobs and in time, he brought most of his extended family—which included three sisters, two brothers, his parents and several in-laws—to live in a large house he found in an Italian enclave in the Bronx. He was eventually able to find work as an artist and textile designer for the French trousseau company, Hermés, putting his artistic talents and training at Brera in Milan to use. He brought embroidery work home from Hermés for his wife, his mother, and his sisters to do. Grace was never asked to help with the fine silk work; they knew she would just make a mess of it with her clumsiness.

Grace's parents were first cousins. They had three children who survived—including her. Armando was her older brother, and Georgio, the younger one. Grace told me her mother had other babies who were born with deformities and didn't live long. Inbreeding is never a good thing.

For a few years, Grace attended a Catholic school in her neighborhood. She had trouble reading and sorting out the English she heard around her from the Italian spoken at home and in the neighborhood shops. The nuns at her school were sharp and called her lazy. They regularly hit her hands with a ruler, and humiliated her when she didn't understand. She didn't easily make friends and so her cousins and extended family were her only companions. After completing the fourth grade—at the age of thirteen, her mother decided Grace was needed at home and so put an end to Grace's formal education. Her father showed her kindness and patience. He took her on outings and gave her an appreciation of art. She adored him.

Grace had odd speech patterns and sometimes difficulty speaking at all, stumbling over words and usually choosing the wrong one. She stuttered at times, and would try to pronounce complicated words using only a syllable or two, not finishing a sentence, assuming the listener understood her intention. I always thought her inability to speak correctly was another sign of her anxiety level; but then, she was always anxious. Many years later, I read about a mental disability that seemed to describe Grace's difficulties in speech as well as her out bursts of rage. But no one ever diagnosed her or found treatment or medication for her. It was just the way she was.

She had no grasp of nuance and so she lacked a sense of humor. With virtually no education, her burgeoning beauty was her only power. As she matured, she became aware of her ability to have doors open for her, sometimes the wrong sort, which she had little sense to differentiate between. By the time she reached her mid-twenties, she had been having an affair with an attorney for a couple of years and one day asked him when they were going to get married. She told me she could still hear his laughter so many years later. Whenever a certain old song came on the radio, she would run and hurriedly turn it off. It was the song playing the night she learned the attorney didn't consider her marriageable material.

Grace met Frank during the Depression, both happy to have jobs during that time. They were working in a department store in Manhattan—she as a salesclerk and he as the manager. She was twenty-eight years old, on the verge of being considered a spinster by her family and society in general in those days. She lived in the northern Bronx with her extended family—sharing the family events, dramas and festivities. Although beautiful, Grace was seen as the dumb one—and, too, there was that temper. She had begun to reconcile herself to the possibility of never marrying. Frank was thirty-six, recently divorced, and living alone in a one-room apartment. Loneliness makes for odd bedfellows.

The walk to Los Arcos was flower-strewn, with blue skies and a light breeze. It was once again a very hot day. There were fields of wheat and plastic covered patches of asparagus. There was, however, no shade and I was relieved to find a grove of trees next to a stream that divided the fields. Walking on a little further, there were signs that someone had been in the wheat field and pressed down the grasses with a tent, probably the night before. I laid down in the soft grass for almost an hour, waving off bugs and flying insects, before giving-up on the idea of sleep and going back into the hot sun.

Although I was always passing or being passed by other pilgrims that I'd met along the way, I missed The Architect's company. The Dutch Couple Who Picnic waved from their shady spot under a tree, well off the path where they were sitting enjoying their lunch. The Mexican Boy Scouts "leader" Marco, stopped to walk with me for a while. The three of them had rescued a record number of people with their remedies for sunburn and blisters. The incessant song of the cuckoo birds that nested in the forests outside of Los Arcos accompanied me for the final hours of my walk.

The town itself arrived abruptly. There were no outlying areas to buffer my approach to the dry and grim hamlet. The Camino markers, which were confusing, finally led me directly onto the main street.

After signing into what I thought was the official, municipal *refugio*, I discovered that it was in fact a private three-story house, owned and managed by a thin and nervous looking couple, Juan and Almeada, who lived in the house with their young daughter. The wife was haggard and irritable and at the same time she wore a stiff, artificial smile. The husband was quiet and did nothing on his own initiative but ran quickly to fulfill whatever task his wife decreed was needed. Their little girl, who looked to be about six years old, followed shyly behind her father.

On the first floor the woman kept a small shop where she sold milk, bread and other staples and also a vast assortment of what looked like day-old pastries and cookies. I hadn't eaten lunch again so I bought bread, wine, anchovies, cheese and a sort of cream puff.

The second and third floor rooms were divided into male and female sleeping rooms with male and female showers. Even married couples were expected to sleep in separate rooms. It was only The Brazilian Brigade who broke rank and decided that the woman in their company had to sleep with them in the men's room because they would all be getting up at five o'clock to leave for the day. Almeada grumbled at the violation.

I chose a bunkbed and settled my things under the bed while I went to take a shower and do my laundry. The only available, and permitted, place to hang clothes to dry was from either of two small devices which were attached to the outside of the two kitchen windows on the second floor. I hung what I could there and hoped that everything wouldn't fall to the ground with the additional weight.

The women's bunkroom was crowded and there was a group of four sitting together on the floor, talking rapidly in Spanish. I dug out the earplugs from my backpack, and laid down to take a nap. As my eyes were closing, I saw a heavy-set, middle-aged woman arrive who had a shaved head and an enormous, metal-framed backpack, loaded with additional equipment—an axe, some pots, a tent roll. She claimed the lower bed on the bunk across from me and sat down on it with a long and wistful sigh as she began to remove braces she was wearing on her knees. There was enormous sadness in her—terrible sadness—and I shivered with the sense of it as I turned over and drifted off.

Our haggard hostess woke me when she stopped into the room to announce that she served a pilgrim's dinner for seven euros. Anyone wanting to have the meal would have to sign the sheet she waved at us and pay the money in advance. As it happened, only three women decided to sign and pay. Thinking it would be nice to have a hot meal and, still feeling groggy with sleep, I ferreted out my money, and made my reservation. The dinner would be served following the Pilgrim's Blessing at the *Iglesia Santa Maria*, the *señora* announced. "Don't be late returning to dinner," she admonished. "It will all be gone and I won't give money back."

The *Iglesia Santa Maria* was to be a highlight of Los Arcos with its reputation for the famous painted organ they have. The figures and heads of singers are beautifully painted in different positions on the pipes of the organ, with the openings in the pipes creating the opened mouths of a singing choir. The overall effect is playful—something I hadn't seen in Spanish art so far.

Since there was still a little time before the Pilgrim's Blessing, I decided to take a walk to find the town *refugio* where The Architect may have stopped. Following directions on Camino signs that then seemed clear to me, I walked through the arch in the main square and crossed the highway, which skirted a small river. I could hear a radio playing in a schoolyard some distance ahead of me and noticed a group of young teens hanging out in the shade of the building. Some were dancing, others were laughing, flirting, and smoking cigarettes as they sat on a short cement wall that encircled the area. The building was no longer used as a school but was in fact the town's *refugio*. The entire schoolyard area was enclosed with chain link fencing and there were many clothes lines filled with laundry drying strung around the grounds surrounding the building. Through the chain link fence I could see The Mexican Boy Scouts giving back massages to pilgrims who were stretched out on picnic tables.

I called out to them, "*Hola!* . . . Marco! Hi! Did you see The Architect today? Is he staying there?"

"*Hola, señora!* No, *señora*, he did not stop here. He walked on," replied Marco, the only one who spoke English.

"Come! Come, I will give you a massage, *señora*," he added, waving his arm toward the gate where I could enter the area.

"No, thanks very much. I want to go to the Blessing. Are you coming?" I replied.

"Oh, *dios, si! Si!*" he said, looking at his watch and hurrying his friends along. "See you there!"

I walked back across the river and along the roadway to the church in the main square with the strains of an American rock song serenading me the entire way back. "*We—are—fam-i-ly—I got all my sistas with me. . .*" The beautiful and serene pilgrim's service at the church was in strong contrast to the blaring sounds coming from the radio in the school yard but in some ways, the message was the same. The painted faces that "sang" rapturously from the organ's pipes were singing another tune but one with the same intent.

I never saw The Architect again.

The next morning I bought some stale cookies and water from the unhappy señora who overcharged for everything. The dinner the night before had consisted of a watery, salty bowl of an egg-drop kind of soup and plain pasta with a glass of wine—"just take one, please!" I walked out of the shop in the pre-dawn light and tried to shake the feeling of stringent limits the place had given me. Leaving Los Arcos, I passed a cemetery with an entranceway that has a saying engraved in Spanish that I was told to watch for. In English it translates to, "I was what you are. You will be what I am."

Although with maturity, I had come to realize that we all have our "story," I was never so aware of it as I was on the Camino. Everyone I met had a story that they told about themselves, some filled with tragedy and sadness, some with hope and optimism, but each person, including Grace and myself, had his or her tale that defined them. The story that we tell has many categories—there are ethnic, cultural and social headings. There are health, abuse, loss, and grief. It all seemed so clear to me that day as I left Los Arcos, if we tell our story long enough, our history, our woes, our hopes and desires, the story becomes who we are. Or what we *think* we are, and why we react the way we do to what we experience. It would be so simple if we could just change our story, become another story—become another Me.

The beauty of the walk that day was dazzling. There were vast fields of wheat rolling on for miles on either side of me and small gatherings of low stone houses and out-buildings that might be called "villages." The sky was incredibly blue and the heat had abated somewhat. On some stretches of the walk, there were boundless fields of

flowers on either side of the path: yellow big-bush flowers, thistles, deep purple and spiky lavender, white margaritas, primrose-like lavender-colored petals with big yellow centers, red and orange poppies, small and delicate pinks and others with lacy yellow petals on tall stalks. The fragrance of them was intoxicating. For hours that morning I didn't hear any kind of machine; neither a tractor nor a car nor even an airplane overhead.

Torres del Rio came and went without my particularly noticing. I stopped to buy some water and continued a short way out of the town to the *Ermita Señora del Poyo* where the virgin of Le Puy had appeared and supposedly left an image of herself. On one side of the path there's a crumbling ruin of a small stone chapel. Vine-covered and desolate looking now, it was built to the Virgin who's associated with the French town of Le Puy. On the other side of the path there's a stone slab table that's all that remains of the shrine to her. I looked for the image of the Virgin that was supposed to have been left those centuries ago but I couldn't make it out no matter how I squinted at the stone. Some pilgrims had left flowers in bunches that were picked along the way. There was also a beautiful white lily—and a banana peel.

Walking on, I passed the Roman settlement of Cornava next to the river of the same name. There wasn't much of it that I could see from the path—just some scattered stones. Their position might have made some sense if I had looked more closely, but with my ever-present concern that I had to keep going, I decided not to stop to investigate. Even though I was feeling stronger and the heat was not as severe as it had been in the days before, the weight on my back and the distance I still had to travel to the *Cruz de Ferro* was always on my mind.

The idea of walking from that day of beautiful landscapes into a large, busy city didn't appeal to me, so I chose to stop for the night in Viana, a few miles before I got to Logroño. The markers crossed a highway that I had been walking next to earlier in the day and climbed a dirt path to the town center.

Walking through the cobbled streets of the old town, I followed the arrows to a *refugio* at the end of the main street. The *refugio* itself was in a renovated monastic building adjacent to the hollowed-out ruins of a church, *Iglesia San Pedro*. To enter, you had to go through a wrought iron gate that gave me the feeling I was truly entering the particular confines of the devout.

The facilities were very comfortable with a large, well-equipped kitchen complete with a table for preparation and enough chairs around to seat six or eight people. The dining room, next to the kitchen, was open and spacious with seating at two or three tables, one large enough for the big tour groups walking together that I had hurried past that day.

Most of the beds were three-tiered bunks all closely fit into several small rooms on two floors. The *Ménage á Trois* arrived shortly after I had signed-in and had my passport stamped. They set themselves up in the same room where I had found a lower deck available. We smiled and nodded heads and the two sisters laughed about something-or-other as they had at Roncesvalles. We all turned then to begin the daily ritual of taking a shower, doing our laundry and taking a nap.

San Pedro's ruins were easily accessed from the *refugio* and most pilgrims had chosen the grassy interior of the church to string their laundry lines from one broken wall to another. Some people sat propped-up against a wall, writing in their journals or reading, sipping a glass of wine they had brought there with them. The views out over the fields in the distance toward Logroño were the quintessence of what I had seen so far of the Spanish countryside. It was comfortable in the late afternoon sun but still very warm and the shade that the ancient structure provided was fully occupied.

The markets were just re-opening for the afternoon and local foods were on display in abundance as I walked down the main street past stalls of vegetables and fruits. I would take advantage of the kitchen facilities at the *refugio* and cook a real "meal." At one of the vegetable markets, I found fresh deep green lettuce and red tomatoes that still felt warm from the sun. Next door, in a store that carried meats, pasta and other household things, there was a glass case with different handmade tortellini—all filled with various local cheeses. I chose one that looked plump and appetizing then asked the patron for a shaker of grated cheese and a bottle of local wine. I knew if I planned to have an early meal, I could avoid the crowds that would invade the kitchen later, all vying for the one available knife, colander or soup spoon.

Most pilgrims leave behind extra food they don't want to carry with them so I expected to find olive oil or salad dressing and probably salt and pepper in the kitchen. Sometimes there's even an unfinished bottle of wine or other delicacies that people don't want to chance spilling in their backpacks. I was sure to have plenty of leftovers myself that I could leave for others so the circle of sharing would be complete for me.

When I entered the kitchen, I was the only one there. I put the bag of groceries down on the table and started to look for a pot, some utensils and a corkscrew. As I was beginning to feel I had things in progress, the shaven-headed woman who walked with knee braces entered the room and nodded. She spoke French and seemed by her gestures to be asking my permission to sit at the end of the table, where she took up writing in her diary. She understood a little English, she said. Pointing to myself, I told her my name and learned that her's was Diana and she was from Quebec. I offered her a glass of wine; we toasted. She went back to writing and I began to slice the tomatoes.

A few minutes passed and the quiet of the room began to feel like a true refuge from the activity I could hear in the rooms beyond and overhead. I looked up in my preparations to see Diana looking at me with tears coming down her cheeks. There was nothing I could say to console her but I was compelled to walk to her end of the table and stroke her back, blindly repeating her name and saying, "I'm sorry. I'm so sorry." She rested her head on her hands on the table in front of her and cried for a minute or so with my hand still stroking her back. When she began to compose herself, I offered her a tissue—she accepted and smiled. She stood up to embrace me, sat down again and went back to writing. I walked to the other end of the table and continued cutting the tomatoes, stirring the tortellini, and sipping my wine.

The morning wind spreads its fresh smell.
We must get up and take that in,
    that wind that lets us live.
Breathe before it's gone.

Rumi

The graceful, arched stone bridge, *Puente de Piedra*, is the very one that medieval pilgrims walked as they crossed the River Ebro and entered the bustling city of Logroño. Somehow crossing these bridges always seemed to put the Camino into perspective for me. It was easy to picture the stream of pilgrims before me who had crossed into or out of the city or town I was just approaching or leaving.

The capitol of the province of La Rioja, Logroño is a little more than five miles (9 km) west of Viana. It was an easy destination for me as I headed out of the *refugio* at dawn. I had planned to visit the *Museo de la Rioja* as well as two notable churches in Logroño that I had read about, so I was looking forward to the cultural day ahead.

As its name implies, the *Museo de la Rioja*, is the regional repository of many objects, both secular and non-secular of all things that have to do with the provincial region of Rioja. Much of the collection in the 18th century Baroque palace, consists of paintings and sculptures from the 12th to the 19th century as well as a "retable," the carved and ornate kind of frame, usually seen at an altar, and some other religious carvings and manuscripts that were saved from abandoned monasteries. I looked forward to seeing the collection of manuscripts there, all scribed by monks in the beautiful uncial script of the Middle Ages. Many of the large format, leather bound books, copied laboriously on sheets of prepared parchment skins could still be found intact in antique shops through out Spain. Most others though, have been scooped up by collectors and antiquarians, disassembled and sold off page-by-page for good profit. The *Museo de la Rioja* has made a great effort to protect the traditional heritage of the region.

After I crossed the bridge, I unbuckled my backpack, lowered it to the ground next to me and dug into a side pocket. I had tucked a brochure about Logroño in there that I had found at the *refugio* the night before. As I remembered, the brochure had a clear map of the city. It took a few minutes to orient myself and realize I was on the *Ruã Vieja*. The street is the main pilgrim's route through Logroño's medieval quarter. It's the road to Logroño's *refugio* as well as the route to its famous Pilgrim's Fountain.

In a 12th century pilgrim's guide, which is a part of the manu-script known as the *Codex Calixtinus*, the pilgrim is advised against drinking the water in the rivers all along the way from Estella:

"All the rivers between Estella and

Logroño have water which brings

death to men and beasts who drink

it, and the fish in these streams are

likewise poisonous."

Pilgrims would have been very relieved to arrive at Logroño and be able to safely drink the water. The fountain is below ground level with steps leading down to it. There's an elaborate roof in the style of a classic Greek temple with inset medallions of heraldic emblems and shields placed in the facade. It's also fitted with dual gleaming brass spigots, which are certainly a more recent addition. No pilgrims were enjoying the water as I stood trying to understand the significance of the decorative shields. Two tourists were taking each other's pictures standing next to the fountain and I offered to take a picture of them together. I decided against tasting the water from the enshrined source and walked on to find a bar open for coffee and something to eat.

It was well past the time when locals would be stopping in for their morning coffee—served up with the gossip and news of the day. The slim, mustached young man behind the counter was wearing a crisp white apron and stood polishing a glass with a clean white cloth. He was unaware that I had entered. His eyes were on the television mounted high on the opposite wall. I stood at the bar and unbuckled the belt of my pack, struggling out of it and lowering it to the floor beside me while I looked up at the scene on the TV. From what I could make of the news story, the Queen of Spain was taking part in a memorial service for several Spanish soldiers who died in a maneuver connected with the war in Iraq. The man behind the counter was startled to see me there and quickly turned to greet me and take my order.

"*Hola! Hola, señora, buenos días!*" he said as he used his white cloth to wipe off the bar where I stood. He shook his head and talked to me about the tragedy unfolding on the screen. Of course, I couldn't understand his words, but I knew what he was saying. "*Si, si,* horrible," was all I could think to say in response.

I ordered a *bocadillo* of fried fish (or so I thought) to have with my frothy *café con leché*. As I waited for the man to prepare it, I was riveted to the television—the first I had seen since starting my walk. Seeing the sadness in the faces of the families who had just lost their children, I began to cry. This was the first of many times to come when I felt I was walking on the path as an observer—I was watching people live their lives, each with its own story, plot, direction, purpose, tragedy, and I began to realize that, to some degree, our lives unfold as if on a path. I began to think of the Camino as a metaphor for life itself. We all follow a path; we get up every morning and decide how we're going to feel about the weather, the sleeping arrangements, the blisters, the injuries—usually without giving much thought to the fact that we could stop and change how we looked at all those things. Yet, all the while, we actually have the opportunity to make another choice. Whether we do or not makes all the difference in how we experience the Camino—or life, for that matter.

After finishing breakfast, which turned out to be a dish of fried fish with several slices of crusty bread and a mound of black baked beans, I bought two bottles of water from the bartender and tucked them into my pack. Heaving it up on my back again, I snapped the belt around my waist and started for the door.

"A dios, señora. Buen Camino!" the bartender called out to me. I turned to see him waving to me with the hand that held his polishing cloth again. It looked like a sign of surrender. I smiled and said, *"Gracias, muchos gracias, señor,"* as I stepped out onto the narrow sidewalk and into the hot sun.

Logroño's *Paseo del Espolon,* has a charming old world feeling—narrow streets, shops and cafes. It does, however, mark the limit of the old and the beginning of the more contemporary Logroño with wide streets and bustling traffic. The modern tempo, with the noise, the smells, the confusion, was in sharp contrast to the peace and the rhythm I had been enjoying. After the quiet of the days before, I found being in the city almost frightening as I was assaulted by people moving quickly passed me along the sidewalks, elbows jostling me in a frenzied rush toward . . . what? Cars raced by most likely hurrying to an important event, an appointment, or maybe just racing home.

I wandered back into the old quarter to visit the *Iglesia Santiago* where I lit another votive candle for Grace. Sitting on a pew to rest and gather my thoughts, the quiet coolness of the atmosphere restored my calm. I leaned forward on the bench with the bulk of my backpack behind me, as if I were kneeling in prayer. Three elderly women were seated a few rows in front of me, all dressed in black with black scarves covering their heads which were all bowed over crossed hands. They looked like three crows all in a line. One woman rose and shuffled to the end of the pew. When she reached the aisle, she turned to face the altar, crossed herself and feebly bent her knee. Her eyes caught mine as she turned and walked toward the pew where I was sitting. When she arrived at my row, she reached into the folds of her dress where she drew out a silver shell hanging alongside a crucifix and stretched it forward for me to see. She gestured, smiled broadly with tight lips and pointed proudly to herself wanting me to know that she, too, had been a pilgrim. I smiled in return and nodded to her as she tucked her shell back inside her dress. *"Buen Camino,"* she said softly and continued slowly along the aisle and out of the church.

The *Iglesia* is a late Gothic church from the 16th century that was built on the foundations of a much earlier one. A nearly life size stat ue of St. James as the slayer of the Moors is set into a deep niche over the massive main door. St James sits astride a powerful looking horse that is as menacing looking as St. James himself. The image of Santiago with his cape covered in shells and his wide-brimmed hat pinned back with a shell is common along the Camino. *Santiago Matamoros,* as the

legend goes, rose up out of the sea on horseback, covered in scallop shells, to aid a bridegroom in great danger of drowning and then later went on to slaughter the invading Moors. The passions of the religious can be vengeful and they seem to find no resolution to their age-old conflicts. The grievances between Christiandom and Islam continue with no resolution in sight.

After leaving the church, I went in search of the *Museo*, following the map I drew from the pocket of my pants. As it happened, the museum was closed for the day—Monday—so, disappointed once again, I decided to get back on the Camino and move on.

I walked briskly on through the city, foregoing the chance to see the other church in Logroño, and crossed a highway where the Camino becomes part of a municipal park. As the walk takes a course through the park and out of the out-lying city, there are benches and playing fields, a snack bar and a large lake.

A group of uniformed school children playing together began to giggle when they saw me approaching on the paved walkway next to the lake. One brave child stepped forward, waved to me and said "*Buen Camino, señora!*" The other children immediately fell into gales of laughter and all of them ran away—trailed by the courageous one.

After leaving the park area, the Camino follows a dirt road that runs next to a wood shredding company on one side and a chain link fence on the other. The fence separates the Camino from a highway down below the hill the path was ascending. Many pilgrims had taken pieces of the wood that was lying about and had fashioned small crucifixes which they then wove into the chain link. Hundreds and hundreds of crucifixes were placed within the fence for the entire stretch of the walk that ran next to and a bit beyond the wood shredding company.

Once the trail reached the countryside, it rambled alongside and often directly through some of the large vineyards that crisscross the province. Many of the vineyard owners were clearly pushing the ancient pathway further and further away from valuable, tillable land. Noticing how the path would at times curve around fields planted with vines, I wondered where the true medieval Camino really was. Generally, for centuries, the route took pilgrims westward—generally over the route so well marked today, but I came to realize that I was not necessarily always placing my foot exactly where pilgrims for centuries before had. Until interest in the pilgrimage to Santiago de Compostela was revived in the late 1970s and early 1980s, mostly through the efforts and support of the British organization, the Confraternity of Saint James, there was little evidence of the Camino in some areas of northern Spain and much of it had to be "reconstructed."

When I reached a slight rise in the rolling fields of La Rioja, the lines and patterns of the planted vineyards were more easily seen. They stretching out endlessly for miles in every direction and the beauty of their design was awe-inspiring, even though the day was hot and dusty. Ochre earth blew up and covered everything—including my boots, clothes, skin, my hat and hair. At one junction on the path, where it crossed a paved road and soon dove back into the vineyards, several men were working in the rows of supported vines. They showed only vague interest in my walking along behind them. One dark-haired young man looked over his shoulder more out of curiosity than any real interest in what I was doing there. He smiled at me, said nothing, then turned and continued his work. The sweltering, unrelieved heat that was building into the day was even more palpable with the lack of shade trees. At times I crossed through fields of fruit trees that went on for miles and miles as the vines had done but they too cast no shade on the path. My thirst was constant and I stopped a couple of times to ferret out the bottle of hot water from my backpack.

Just outside of Navarette are the remains of the Romanesque hospital of St.John of Acre (founded in the late 1100s). Built as a hostel and infirmary for the early pilgrims, the ruins have been somewhat restored. I enjoyed standing there and imagining the building when it was bustling with pilgrims as the present-day *refugios* are. The shade was of even more interest though, as it was to several other pilgrims who stopped to rest after the shadeless walk of the day. Pilgrims always greet each other with a nod and a *"Hola!"* and those few who were resting did so to me as I stripped off my backpack and found a spot to sit.

Three young women speaking Spanish were arguing about something. They looked very hot and tired. One was limping and didn't want to leave the rest stop as the others rose to move on. Two older men sat on the ground sharing a bottle of wine and laughing. Four or five slim men in tight-fitting bicycling pants and shirts stood with their bikes propped against their well-muscled bodies as they swigged from the plastic water containers that fit onto the frames of their bicycles.

"Excuse me, Madame," said a tall young man who took off his hat and made a slight bow. He spoke very formal British English with a slight accent that I took to be Dutch.

"Are you The American Woman Who is Carrying Her Mother?" he asked.

"Well, yes," I said, "I guess I am." I was puzzled that he would know me—or at least who I was.

"I am very glad to meet you. I bring greetings from The Savior," he explained. (*Really? The real one?*, I laughed to myself.) "I met him yesterday on the path where I had stopped to rest outside of Los Arcos. He asked if I had seen you. He was concerned that you were doing alright and asked if I would look out for you."

"Oh, my goodness. I'm very touched. That's very nice of him—and of you. Yes, I'm doing quite well actually. Thank you."

"Alright, then. When I see him next I will give him the good news of your progress, Madame." With that, he put his rumpled blue cotton hat back on, seemed to offer another gesture that certainly looked like a bow to me, and turned to rejoin the path.

"Buen Camino," he called out as he turned back towards me and waved. People were often looking out for one another on the trail. It was very comforting to know that.

When I woke up that morning I had a delicious feeling of comfort and ease. It was surprising that I felt that way simply because most of the time I was physically uncomfortable sleeping in those dormitory-like rooms. The beds were narrow, there was always far too much activity going on, day and night. Rooms often smelled of the multitude of people sharing them and "quiet" was a relative term.

That particular morning, however, I lay in bed, not thinking of "getting moving," or the miles ahead of me or my goal for the day. I was basking in a kind of pleasure I felt from—what? In an instant, I remembered a dream I was having just as I woke. It was about Grace. I was quickly losing the thread of what the dream was about but I held onto the feelings I was left with, much the way we do when we wake from a bad dream. We're often not sure of why we're frightened but the feeling is there nevertheless. In the dream I saw Grace's face, which looked almost beatific and she was being uncharacteristically loving and comforting to me. She had her arms wrapped around me and hugged me close as one might hold a baby. She stroked my hair and kissed me on my forehead. I heard her cooing, "I love you, precious child." I have no memory of her ever having said those words to me. I suppose it really doesn't matter when they come. They were so warmly welcome.

I dug into one of the outside pockets of my backpack and retrieved my journal. I hadn't written in it for a few days and I wanted to be sure to remember some of the events of the days before. I did a few drawings from memory of the "Crucifix of the Chain Link," the fields of vineyards, and the building in front of me. After what seemed like an hour, I realized I had to move on to be sure to arrive at the *refugio* in Navarette before all the beds were taken.

Navarette appeared in the distance sometime toward the middle of the day. The red/ocher colored town was built close up against a hill of the same color. The town and area around it is known for the pottery made of the clay found in the area. As I followed the painted yellow arrows and scallop shell markers toward the *refugio*, I passed a few pottery shops with the owners' wares in the windows. In one shop, I saw a potter busy at his wheel. It was tempting to think about buying a small piece, but I reconsidered, knowing it would add to the weight I was carrying and would likely get broken long before I reached Santiago.

Navarette had a narrow, three-story *refugio* facing directly onto a narrow cobbled street, next to a bar. As I approached, I saw some pilgrims sitting at small tables gathered outside the bar while others were hanging their pants, shirts and underwear on the town wall across from the building. The wind swept up the dry red dust from the street and covered the wet clothes in a gritty haze. Some people walked from the *refugio* up the narrow winding street with their dripping laundry to the town steps that led to the top of the hill above the *refugio*. I was told that they had created a network of clotheslines where their billowing clothes caught the wind and dried almost instantly.

The *refugio* was very crowded. Some young people had noisily taken over the third floor and word went out that they were planning a birthday party. All the beds on the second floor were taken but one and luckily I was able to claim it with my backpack, get my boots off, gather my toiletries and quickly step into the line forming for a shower. There was just enough room left to hang my laundry in an open window opposite my bunk.

For a few days after leaving Los Arcos, I hadn't seen anyone I knew earlier on the path with the exception of Diana from Quebec. Though we'd never had any conversation, in the usual sense, there had clearly been a bond between us that day in the kitchen at Viana. Diana was quiet and I think she was very shy. She didn't talk to even the French- speaking pilgrims who tried to engage her. She always walked alone. Here at Navarette, following the ritual afternoon *siesta*, we greeted each other and sat together at a table outside the bar next to the *refugio*. Diana was once again writing in her journal and I sat drinking a cold beer from a tall glass, eating some chips, doing some drawings and watching the street scene. Local people were walking hurriedly along, carrying open-mesh shopping bags filled with greens or breads; pilgrims were standing together in groups, sharing stories, laughing, or consulting their guidebooks. Some were looking for space to hang their laundry on the town wall. Those pilgrims just arriving, were walking slowly up the street, some leaning heavily on their walking sticks, looking solemn and exhausted.

A specially priced pilgrims' dinner was being offered that evening in a small restaurant in the main plaza. Diana and I joined some others who had decided to have the hot meal. We strolled slowly down a narrow street past still more pottery shops and across the plaza which fronted an ornate late Gothic church. As we entered the restaurant we were greeted by a short, burly man who directed us to a room at the back of the building. Several large framed photos of bull fighters spearing their respective bulls, hung on the walls of the otherwise colorless room we were relegated to. A large television was set up on a table at one end of the room. Word went around that we were to have the special treat of watching the bullfights being televised from Madrid while we had our dinner. They were about to begin.

Two groups of several local men also crowded into the room, each man holding a glass of the deep red local wine in thick rough hands. They all wore dark beret-like hats, simple shirts, open at the collar, and course dark pants. They settled around the tables closest to the TV screen and all put money in a pile in the middle of the table.

Our first course of soup was served just as the bullfight began. I have no memory of what the rest of the dinner consisted of after the soup of greens. The meal was a blur to me as I hurried through it to escape the enforced viewing of the massacre. I excused myself and made my way back to the *refugio* alone.

Lying in my bunk later, I tried to erase the images of the bullfight on the TV screen. Instead, I shifted my annoyance and horror to a man in the room I referred to as "Naked Nils." Hanna had once told me I was a prudish American. "*Ya*, you people are always so careful not to show your body!" she had said when she saw me struggling to cover myself after a shower. I had never thought of myself as prudish. Naked Nils, though, did embarrass me with his nudity. He seemed to enjoy his fine physique and walked around the bunkroom in his very scant underwear without even the slightest bit of self-consciousness or awareness that parts of his private parts weren't really very private.

As he stood combing his hair in the one communal mirror, I felt very uncomfortable and decided then and there that I didn't like him. I was lying in my bunk, trying to sleep with my earplugs in, thinking solely about this particular man (whom I didn't know at all) and listing all of the things I didn't like about him as he walked back and forth past my bunk. I could have closed my eyes or turned toward the wall but I was looking for justification for my feelings.

My quick and stern judgment of him was too harsh by far—as such irrational bigotry always is. It was my own discomfort that caused me to judge him so ruthlessly. And so, Hanna was once again right—this time about my prudishness. Less than a week later in Santo Domingo de la Calzada, Naked Nils was to show himself to be a deeply caring and selfless person.

You're crying. You say you've burned yourself.
But can you think of anyone who's not
hazy with smoke?

Rumi

The next day I got an unusually early start. So many others were
getting up, shuffling around in the room, and walking out in the pre-
dawn darkness that I decided rather than trying to sleep a
little more—at least until dawn—I'd get started on the day's walk. The
early hours were definitely cooler and I might possibly be able to go a
little further if I didn't get so depleted by the heat.

The markers lead me on through the quiet streets of Navarette
with only the foot sounds of two pilgrims walking along in front and
two or three behind me. The small village of Ventosa was the first I
passed through. It was still shuttered in the soft morning light. No bars
were open for coffee and the town held no particularly significant
church for me to stop to see so I continued on with Nájera as my next
goal. Leaving Ventosa behind, no other pilgrims were in sight for as far
as I could see in the low light. None trailed me either, so I enjoyed the
quiet solitude of the morning.

Along that stretch of the Camino massive nests of sticks and limbs
are constructed on top of church steeples, bell towers, water towers and
any other imaginable high place—even atop stanchions carrying electric
power lines. The nests were those of immense white storks. The species

of stork that nests in northern Spain builds its nests near people rather than in the woods as do other storks. Generations of the birds return to Spain to reproduce every spring. They make the long journey from North Africa to take up residence sometimes in the same nest year after year. Just outside of Nájera I saw two, or possibly three nests in the same bell tower. There was little room for the bell to chime and, if and when it did, there would be many sleepless stork babies.

No villages interrupted the eight or nine mile stretch between Ventosa and Nájera. The path followed right next to a main highway for some of the way and then crossed it and returned to the vineyards again only to skirt and cross the highway still again. It was obvious that the vineyard owners wanted us off their land and away from their grapes.

Walking on a long section of dirt path that swept through the vine-yards like a russet ribbon, I could see Nájera long before it arrived. The town is built up against a large hill of red rock, much like Navarette, and as I got closer, Nájera appeared more elegant architecturally. The old quarter is easily reached by crossing the River Nájerilla on yet another ancient, low-arched bridge.

Until the death of Sancho IV, king of Navarra, who was murdered by Alphonso VI king of Castile in 1076, Nájera had been the seat of the royalty of the Rioja and Navarra provinces. Nájera's position and prominence on the Camino was made secure by the maneuverings of Sancho III who, in the mid-11th century, altered the route to pass through the city rather than around it. Interestingly, I thought about how today vineyard owners are altering the route for their own inter-ests as well.

The *Monasterio de Santa Maria la Real*, built in the same century as Sancho's redirection of the Camino, is still a functioning monastery that dominates the town's landscape. The monastery itself is situated right at the river's edge and the building became a resting place for almost thirty royals of the families of the provinces of Navarre, as well as some of those from Castile and León.

On entering the side door of the monastery, I was drawn to the beautiful inner cloister with its late Gothic tracery style known as Plateresque. The cloister was added in the 15th century and is called the Cloister of the *Caballeros* (knights) because of the number of royals and nobles buried there. As I walked around the sheltered corridor-like space, looking toward the central garden area, the compelling strains of Gregorian chants echoed through the building. After making a complete circle around the entire cloister, opening any unlocked doors I passed, I stood in frustration at the spot where I had started. Standing there, trying to see if I could figure out where the monks were singing, I heard electrical static. Looking up in the direction of the sound, I spotted a speaker and then another and another.

Giving up my fruitless search for live singing monks, I went instead to look for the monument to Blanca, wife of Sancho III, who died in 1158. According to legend, King Don Garcia ordered construction of the monastery and church after the Virgin appeared to him in a cave. The cave is included as part of the crypt in the lower level of the building, along with the mausoleum of the Dukes of Nájera. Signs indicated I'd find Blanca there.

The stone-sculpted tomb, showing Blanca lying as if in sleep on the top of the sarcophagus, seemed timeless. I was intrigued by the details of her gown, her hair, headpiece and her jewelry. Several other tombs of nobles, were all in a row; kings and queens sleeping together in the quiet of the dimly lit room. It gave me an odd, somewhat discomforted feeling. How differently we all deal with death—then and now.

The diversion to visit the monastery was very refreshing. I walked around Nájera's old quarter and found a small store where I bought some yogurt, fruit and water then went to the river to sit in the shade and enjoy my picnic. Stretching out on the grass, with my head on my backpack, I looked up through the trees and almost fell asleep as I lay dreaming lazily of knights, queens and other such nobles.

When I next saw them, Hanna and Horst were sitting at a table in a bar in Azofra; a small ochre town perched on a hill a few miles before the Camino reaches Santo Domingo de la Calzada. The bar, which faces the *Plaza de Fuente*, seemed to be a favorite of pilgrims. Probably the fact that it was the only place in town to get something to eat had a great deal to do with that.

All of the small wooden tables were crowded with people—some talking, laughing and others more somberly sitting just quietly eating. Two young plump, dark haired girls, both with furrowed brows, bustled around the room, carrying trays of food and drinks—clearing here, taking orders there. Backpacks and walking sticks were leaning against the walls and propped against chairs. As I entered, I saw Hanna standing and waving with both arms, one hand holding a glass of wine, as she called out to me to join them.

"No, no, don't sit down! Here, leave your pack here and go. Go! Go now to the *refugio* to see if there is any space left. Hurry! See if you can fit—then you come back. *Ya?*"

I unbuckled my backpack and lowered it slowly to the floor, resting it against the wall near their table. Hanna shooed me along with a wagging hand. As I steadied myself on the back of a chair at their table for a moment, she explained why she felt there was such urgency that I hurry to the *refugio*.

"We arrived a little time before, and we have the last beds inside. Maybe there will be a place for you on the porch. We wait here. *Go!*"

Indeed, Hanna proved to be right—all the available beds in the small stone structure were taken and the covered porch attached to the chapel next to the *refugio* was filled to capacity as well. There were mats laid out on the floor of the porch with bedrolls side-by-side covering the mats and the entire surface of the porch. People had purposefully placed their packs well inside from the edge. It looked like there might be a thunderstorm later.

I walked slowly back to the bar with thoughts about what I could do to find a place to sleep that night. My legs were very tired and my knees felt particularly stiff. Stopping at the main crossroads in the village I looked up and down the one dusty main street. There were no signs for a hostel or a privately owned *refugio* or even rooms to rent. I decided to have something to eat and talk to the other pilgrims at Hanna and Horst's table about what my options might be.

Settling into a chair with the four other pilgrims who had joined Hanna and Horst, introductions went around the table. We all spoke English, for my benefit no doubt, even though one couple was German and the two men were French. I ordered a glass of the regional Rioja white wine from the young waitress who soon arrived at our table. I needed time to think about what I wanted to eat—I was getting tired of eggs with potatoes and *bocadillos* with eggs and cheese. Horst silently held up a basket of bread for me and I bit hungrily into a piece of the fresh crusty *pan*. The soft-faced young woman who bent to wipe the table clean with one hand, collected empty dishes with the other, and nodded as everyone, in unison it seemed, asked for something more to eat or drink. She got it all.

Hanna talked about what my alternatives were for the night. "Well, we could ask if anyone in the *refugio* has a tent. *Ya*! That's what we must do! Maybe someone who is sleeping inside has a tent for you!" she was excited to have found a solution so quickly.

As we sat chatting and I asked the pilgrims seated around us if anyone had a tent, I was beginning to feel very stiff and I fidgeted in my chair, trying to shake the feeling off. I attempted to stand up and realized that *I couldn't move my legs!* I had walked one hundred and twenty-five miles and my knees had clearly had enough. Looking down at them now, it was obvious even through my long pants, they had become very swollen. Every part of my body ached.

Our waitress had told the woman at the bar that I needed a room. The barmaid then called out to one of the French pilgrims at our table, who spoke fluent Spanish, that her mother had a room upstairs where I could stay the night. Everyone seemed in on the arrangements.

A short, plump woman with jet-black hair and a broad smile pushed through the swinging doors from the kitchen behind the counter. She rounded the corner at the end of the bar, wiping her hands on her apron, and walked up to our table. She stretched out her hand to shake mine and spoke very slowly in Spanish in an effort to help me understand her. There was no need though—the Frenchman at my table and other pilgrims at surrounding tables were all interpreting for me. The whole group of seven or eight translators began to laugh and enjoy the "committee" effect of their efforts as I looked from one to the other and became more and more confused. Finally, Hanna took over in her usual way, and confirmed the available bed upstairs in the same building in a shared room with another woman and the price of twelve euros for the night.

Since the hotelier was ready with her keys to lead me to the room, I said good-bye to the others with many *"Buen Camino"*s shared back and forth. Lifting my backpack in my arms, and hugging it at my chest, I shuffled along, following the *señora* out the front door. We turned left and walked a few steps to another door that opened onto an entryway with stairs to the rooms above.

I managed to get up the stairs by sitting down on one step backwards and raising my rear end up onto the step above. Unfortunately, the room I was to rent was on the third floor. I had to leave my backpack in the entryway where the *señora* assured me it would be safe. Once at the top, I hobbled down the hallway, bracing

myself on the walls, to where my hostess was standing, waiting to show me the room. As she knocked lightly and then opened the door, she stood gesturing into what seemed to be little more than a walk-in closet. The room was just large enough to fit two narrow beds end-to-end with a small passageway between them.

The other bed in the room was occupied by a tall and very large young German girl who boomed a greeting to me in English and immediately returned to reading her guidebook. With clear annoyance, she placed her book down on the floor next to her bed, breathed a deep sigh, heaved herself up and reluctantly consented to retrieve my backpack at the bottom of the stairs.

The *señora* then pointed out a bathroom on the other side of the hallway that I was anxious to use. As we continued with our tour, I was able to gather from her few words of English and mine of Spanish that there was a young Austrian family with two small children who had taken the room next to the bathroom. Finally, turning around to the doorway at the end of the hallway, she pointed to the small kitchen with cook stove. It was taken over with dinner preparations that the family had in progress. Even though it was a highly inflated price, I nodded that the room would be fine and happily paid her the twelve euros for a place to lie down. Most rates for accommodations at the pilgrim's *refugios* were in the range of three or four euros.

There were far too many times when I found myself with no food and no way of getting any at the end of the day. I felt I was a complete failure as a long-distance walker. Always conscious of adding weight to my load, when I did find a market open, I bought only the minimum—just enough to quell the hunger I felt at the moment, not enough for the hunger that would revisit later. Here I was again with no food and in too much pain to try to get back down the stairs to the bar to order something to eat and then get back to my room again. I briefly thought of asking my roommate if she would buy me something to eat with my few remaining euros but I reconsidered when she threw my pack on the bed and stomped off down the hall.

Pushing my pack aside, I sat down on the edge of the bed and took off my boots. With a deep sigh, I allowed the exhaustion and disappointment to wash over me. As I held my head in my hands, I let the tears flow. They came in waves that wracked my body as I heaved and sunk into the pain I was feeling—both physical and emotional.

CARRYING GRACE TO SANTIAGO

The pain in my body was excruciating, I could hardly catch my breath. I was overwhelmed with grief at the thought that I might not be able to walk any further and that in fact, as some people in the bar downstairs insisted, I may have permanently damaged my knees. How would I ever get to the *Cruz de Ferro*—nearly two hundred miles away—to leave Grace's ashes? Why was I doing this anyhow? What did I have to prove? Couldn't I have just gone on a nice, leisurely walk across Spain as I first intended to do? But, no, I had to bring her ashes with me and now I've got to go through with it. What in the world was I trying to prove! Was it so important that I do this "heroic" act for Grace—who would probably not care at all about the whole damn thing? Was I still trying to show her I was worthy? I would never know why she put me and my brother in that orphanage now and where the hell was my father then, anyhow? Some questions would have to remain unanswered and what was walking 500 miles going to do to change history? Damn it! I heaved and sighed and cried some more and wiped my shirtsleeve across my eyes.

I raised my wide pant legs to look at my knees and through the haze of my tear-filled eyes, was shocked at their size. They had swollen to two or three times their natural girth and looked very much like cantaloupes! All the planning, all the "training" I had done for months before leaving home was for nothing! With an overwhelming sense of defeat, I fell back on the bed, raised my feet to rest them next to my backpack and slept straight through until morning.

It was arranged in the bar downstairs, even before I maneuvered my way down the steps the next morning, that I should be taken to the part convent/part hostel run by Cistercian nuns in Santo Domingo. Several pilgrims had asked the waitress where I could go to rest for a few days and she made the suggestion and arranged for the taxi. I had very little cash left and with no cash machines in Azofra, I was concerned about how I would pay the man for the ride to Santo Domingo.

Diana from Quebec, who was sitting alone at a table in the bar, overheard the others talking about my predicament, and quietly stood up to approach me. She reached into her pocket to get the twenty or thirty euros they had decided I would need for the taxi and at least one night with food. She had no assurance that I would ever see her again to repay her but it didn't seem to matter. She pushed the bills into my hand and put her arms around me, kissed me on both cheeks and repeated. "Is okay. Is okay. *Bon Camino*, my friend." The sense of camaraderie and caring was so deeply touching. Everyone (except of course the one young woman I shared my room with the night before) was enormously supportive and helpful. They all wanted me to make it—to fulfill my destination, to "win" in whatever way I thought of winning.

I arrived at the *hospitaleria* in Santo Domingo de la Calzada, having been driven from Azofra by a local man who maintained a part-time taxi service. He had a Mercury station wagon that allowed me to lie prone in the back since I wasn't able to sit upright with my knees bent. It was unusual to see such a big American car in the countryside of northern Spain and I smiled at the idea of "Mercury" carrying me away just as I had at "Horace" (Oracio—The Architect) having been my early guide and companion.

The drive was pleasant as I lay looking out the windows at the cloudless blue sky. I thought about the idea that, if the Camino was a metaphor for life itself, as I was beginning to see it, wouldn't it be wonderful if we all treated each other with the kindness I saw on a daily basis as I walked that path.

The driver helped me out of the car and carried my backpack into the building. *"Buen Camino, señora,"* he said as he saluted me, reached for the bills I held out to him, and briskly walked back to his car. After I registered with the woman at the desk who made an effort to speak to me in English, a young nun picked-up my backpack and accompanied me to a tiny elevator that took us to the third floor. When she had opened the door to the small room she quietly put my pack down on the floor next to the bed and turned to leave with a signal that she would be back. A few minutes later, she brought me a sweet roll with a spoonful of jam and a pat of butter on a dish and a cup of hot coffee; my first food since sometime the day before.

The ivory white walls of the room were no more than six or seven feet apart and about twice that distance in length. A narrow bed, pushed against the long wall, was made up with thin pale sheets that had lost their crispness long ago. A soft pale blue cotton blanket covered the bed and another was folded at the bottom of it. Though old, the linens were clean and fresh, as was everything in the room and the adjoining small bathroom. The brown tiled floors gleamed with the years—perhaps centuries—of diligent care and polish.

A short, heavy porcelain tub in the bathroom which was more like a "bathing chair", served as a bathtub. One had to sit in it on a raised platform that was a molded part of the tub. That first day I wasn't able to take advantage of soaking my sore muscles because my knees wouldn't bend to take the seated position. When I had eaten, once again I fell into a deep sleep for almost the entire rest of the day.

The next day I was sitting on a straight-backed wooden chair that was pulled up to a narrow writing desk opposite the bed. I had also been able to immerse myself in the short bathtub, and relished feeling truly clean for the first time since I started the walk. Gripping the walls as I went, I shuffled my way down the hall to the dining room where I had a Spartan luncheon of watery vegetable soup, slightly stale bread and a steamed piece of white fish. My first real meal in days—it was delicious!

Except for an attractive young Spanish couple who sat at a table opposite mine, most of the eight or ten others in the room were elderly women. I mistakenly sat at a table nearest the door when I entered the dining room the first time and with much flurry and bluster, I was asked to move to another table by one of the women who served the meals. That table was always kept for an elderly priest who, along with the ladies, was in residence at the *hospitaleria*. All of the white-haired, bent and black-clad ladies sat in complete silence at every meal—even the young couple, who whispered to each other from time-to-time, seemed very solemn.

Occasionally I would pass a gnome-like man in the halls as I went to and from the dining room. It seemed his job was to fix things around the building—the electricity was always going out, something always needed to be painted . . . grumble, grumble, grumble. He wore wheat-colored overalls over a wrinkled short-sleeved blue shirt and carried a ladder twice as long as he was tall. He walked in a determined manner with his head down, mumbling. The *señora* I met at the desk on my first day usually asked about my knees. I could understand only three or four of her words but her gentle, caring manner was clear in her eyes and her smile. She wrote things down for me in English. I wrote down questions for her in Spanish (which I looked-up in my Spanish phrase book). By the end of my stay, when I was able to walk and in doubt of her directions, she would walk out of the building with me to show me the right direction.

Back in my room after lunch on the third day, I was sitting at the desk, drawing and writing in my journal, and paused to look over my shoulder toward the small window to the left of the bed. The thin colorless curtains fluttered in the warm afternoon breeze that came from the shaded garden at the back of the building. A large wooden cross hung on the wall over the bed with the body of Jesus draping limply from it. On the wall in front of me above the writing desk, was a framed print of a human heart with a crown perched on the top of it. Thorns pierced the heart and blood dripped from it.

Rising from the garden below, came the sound of laughter and familiar voices.

...but don't be satisfied with stories, how things
have gone with others. Unfold your own myth,
without complicated explanation,
so everyone will understand the passage,
We have opened you.
Start walking toward Shams. Your legs will get heavy
and tired. Then comes a moment of feeling
the wings you've grown, lifting.

Rumi

Aﬁter hobbling over to the window, I looked down and through the tree branches below to an adjacent garden. Several people were sitting on chairs randomly arranged on a stone patio. A few backpacks rested along the wall that surrounded the garden. The sounds of music playing on a radio, people chatting and laughing wafted up to me. I realized that I was looking onto the back garden of the main refugio in Santo Domingo.

The familiar voices I heard were those of The Mexican Boy Scouts and I could just see the tops of their three jet black heads as they sat softly laughing and talking together. I wanted so much to run downstairs and around the block to see them. At least to call out and say "Hey, Mexican Boy Scouts, up here! *Hola!* Hi, how are you?" but thought better of it, knowing the nuns would most likely ask me to leave after such an outburst in their quiet, solemn residence.

The next day I heard Hanna talking and that afternoon, I saw The Dutch Couple Who Picnic sitting together reading. The three days I had spent resting had been peaceful and restorative but I was beginning to realize that if I was going to move on, I had better get going. Watching the other pilgrims from my window gave me a yearning to be a part of the adventure again. The first thing I needed to do was to see if I could make it out to the street to find a banking machine; get some money; see if I could find Diana from Quebec to pay her back the money she gave me; and maybe look for an internet cafe to write friends and family.

A few minutes later, and without too much difficulty, I was standing on the sidewalk in front of the *hospitaleria*. Looking up and down the street for a bank with a machine that was close-by, I saw The Dutch Couple Who Picnic approaching.

"So, you have made it after all! Good for you! We heard you had left the walk and were going home," said the elderly Dutchman. He and his wife (who didn't speak English) seemed genuinely delighted to see me.

They were both tall, tan and looked very fit. My impression was that they did this sort of thing all the time—walked together or at least spent a great deal of their time together outside. They walked, camped, picnicked together with such ease and obvious comfort, everyone who spoke of them thought they were such a perfectly happy couple. They both dressed well in clothes that looked especially made for serious camping and hiking. They had well-made backpacks and excellent, expensive Italian walking boots. I never met them at a *refugio* even though we often passed on the trail. I learned later that they usually stayed in pensions or small hotels where they could get a better sleep and have some privacy.

"No, no—not leaving yet! I've been resting here for a few days." We shook hands and smiled warmly at one another. Clearly, they saw me as a part of their walk, just as they were a meaningful part of mine. One's presence in someone else's story makes a difference to them just as theirs does to us, though we seldom realize it at the time.

"I'm thinking of spending another day or two here then taking a bus to Burgos and I'll see how I feel then. I'd like to get back to actually walking the Camino again. It doesn't feel right to travel by bus."

"Oh, well, don't worry about that, dear. Even in the middle ages, the pilgrims hopped on the back of carriages and carts. They rode horses and hitched rides whenever they could!" he said encouragingly.

To save me some steps, The Couple suggested they would walk around the nearby streets to see where the closest banking machine was from where I was standing. They returned in a couple of minutes and pointed me in the right direction down the main street. We once again waved our *"Buen Camino"*s and *"Ultreya"*s and went our separate ways.

With cash in my pocket, I decided to reward myself for getting out of bed, making the effort to move, and generally for just being somehow deserving of an eatable reward. A piece of fruit or cheese or a good loaf of bread didn't appeal to me. Since I had been eating those sorts of things for days, I wanted something completely extravagant to have as my treat. There was a bakery next to the cash machine and the window displayed an enticing variety of delicious-looking sugary confections. I spent a few minutes trying to make up my mind as to which ones would be most delicious and finally walked in and selected two luscious chocolaty pastries. I asked the man behind the counter for some milk to go with my feast and was able to make out that he had no milk left—only cream to wash down my goodies. Grasping the bag he handed to me and a few paper napkins he offered, I turned and walked slowly out to a bench in a nearby plaza.

Three young women were gathered on a bench across from mine. Carriages and children's toys—stuffed animals and dolls surrounded them. They were talking quietly together while their young toddlers played nearby. The children looked so beautiful as they sat together on the smooth stones of the plaza. Occasionally one would jump up, shrieking with joy. They ran around the bench where their mothers sat and they giggled over unknown, unseen dangers. I was touched by their sweetness and their obvious sense of security and happiness. The entire world was safe for them—and, if sometimes it didn't quite feel that way, there was someone to love them and hold them and tell them that all would be okay again in a moment or two. They giggled and laughed at everything that one or the other of them did. I began to laugh along with them as I sat eating my cream-filled feast. Lost in the pleasure of their company, I was startled when Naked Nils approached.

"*Hola!* What is this?" he said, pointing to my legs. "I'm glad to see you! You have had a difficult time, no? I heard you hurt your leg, yes?" He stretched out both of his hands to grasp mine between them. I quickly wiped my pant leg with the sugar, cream and chocolate and extended mine. He was very handsome, tall and tanned. He stood straight and spoke with a clipped, precise accent. His compassion seemed sincere.

"No, it was just my knees—and I think a bit of just plain exhaustion. I've been sleeping and sleeping and sleeping for the last couple of days. My knees still feel pretty stiff and I've been trying to figure out what to do next. I don't want to quit. I have to get to the *Cruz de Ferro* at least."

"Oh, yes, I heard this. You will put your mother's ashes there, yes?"

"Well, that was my plan but I just don't know now . . . "

"Oh, you must make it! I will help you!" he said excitedly. "I am going to take the bus tomorrow back to Logroño where my friend has left his car. I'll get the car and come for you here. We are going to Burgos, León and Astorga. We can take you as far as Astorga. That will help, no?"

My eyes filled with tears and I almost lost my breath. I had been feeling very emotional and vulnerable in the last few days and every kindness seemed to overwhelm me. I turned to where he now sat next to me on the bench and embraced him. I was touched that he was willing to come back to Santo Domingo and drive me another hundred miles or so further toward the *Cruz de Ferro* just to help me leave Grace. He didn't know me, we had never spoken before and the last thoughts I had of him were very judgmental. I was humbled by his kindness. Indeed, his offer was another example of how everyone walking the Camino wanted to help everyone else reach their goal. It mattered little whether another pilgrim was known or not—we were all on the path and everyone's travel had meaning.

"No, I couldn't possibly ask you to do that!" I choked out. "I can't tell you how much I appreciate your offer but there's a part of me that would feel that I had given up on my idea of actually carrying Grace's ashes myself if we (Grace and me) just got in the back of your car and zipped across the countryside at 70 miles an hour. I just need a little more time to heal and I'll try to get back to walking again."

We sat on the bench in the shade of the plaza talking for a while, with the sound of the children's laughter ringing like bells chiming all around us. We compared stories of our experiences on the path and motives for making the walk—as all pilgrims do. His name was Alexander and I told him that Alessandra was my middle name and went on to tell him my "name story." I was still finding ways to tell people about all the crazy things that Grace did—justifying my grievances.

"Oh, yes, we might have had the same name!" I explained. "Alexander / Alessandra—but for a last minute change Grace made while she was in labor giving birth to me. She was lying in a bed, next to a woman who had just been wheeled back to the ward after having given birth to a stillborn baby. The woman was crying and Grace asked her why and the woman, with a thick Irish brogue, explained that her baby girl had not lived and that she had planned to name her Maureen."

"For whatever reason," I went on, "Grace told the woman that if she had a girl, she would name her Maureen. So, much to my father's surprise, the name I was given was Maureen and the name they had agreed upon became my middle name." We both laughed at the ludicrous way the choice was made. My name had always been for me another example of Grace's impetuous nature and her inappropriate alliances. Alexander thought it was very kind of her to care so much about the woman's loss and that maybe I should think of it that way.

Alexander was in a supervisory position as a social worker in a city near Frankfurt. He was making the walk with a young man who worked for him that he was enamored of and hoped to make a more meaningful relationship with by sharing the experience of the Camino. It was the young man, Richard's, car that they would retrieve the following day. If he couldn't help me get to the *Cruz de Ferro*, he and his friend would likely visit the *Monastario de Santo Domingo de Silo* south of Santo Domingo before driving on to Astorga.

The Benedictine monks of that monastery broke world records when their recordings of Gregorian chants hit the charts in the mid-1990s. A friend of mine who was living in Madrid at the time had sent me two tape cassettes of the stunning music and I had planned to visit the monastery in the hopes of actually hearing the monks sing—live! The beauty of the Romanesque cloister there is often heralded for the very unusual carvings on the capitals, which top the many columns of the enclosure. Still more enticing to me though was the chance to see the 11th century, *Missal of Silos*, which is the oldest manuscript written on paper in the Western world. The document is made up of over 150 folios, which are kept in the library at the monastery. It looked like the monastery, however, would have to be part of another trip for me. I had lost so much time that I felt I couldn't afford to take any side trips that would take me added days to walk and put more stress on my body.

The next day I woke feeling somewhat stronger and eager to see some of Santo Domingo. After making a brief stop in the solemn dining room, where I had a cup of milky coffee and a crusty roll, I headed to the elevator. Once out on the street, I breathed in the fresh morning air, feeling a wonderful sense of freedom—being about to walk around without my backpack strapped on! Slowly I wandered off in the direction of the cathedral famous for its chickens.

Santo Domingo de la Calzada was a major stopping place for early pilgrims traveling to Santiago and it continues to be a favorite town for pilgrims and tourists alike. The bridge that crosses the *Rio Oja*, for which the province was named, was built for the pilgrims by a hermit who later became a monk of no particular order (although he's sometimes referred to as a Benedictine). Dominic was eventually revered as a saint for his dedication to the pilgrims and for making their passage easier by building roads and bridges from Logroño to Burgos. He built a church, and a hospital, which is now a beautifully restored, State-owned luxury hotel, or *parador*, in Santo Domingo as well as some of the roads outside the town. The roadways are the source of the town's name—"Saint Dominic of the Causeway,"

Santo Domingo de la Calzada, however, is best known for an event that legend says took place there sometime during the middle ages, involving an early pilgrim who caught the eye of a young maiden of the town. As the story goes, a man and woman and their handsome young son were on their way to Santiago and stopped in Santo Domingo to rest. The handsome pilgrim rebuffed the maiden's advances and she sought revenge by placing some coins in his bag and pointing to him as a thief. He was condemned and hanged. His parents sadly continued their pilgrimage to Santiago and on their return, they went to the gallows and prayed for their son's soul. Much to their happy surprise, their son was alive (through the intervention of St. Dominic) and he implored them to go to the judge and plead to have him cut down.

When the couple appealed to the judge at his home, he was about to sit down to a meal of roasted chicken. In disbelief that the young man could possibly still be alive, the judge laughed and said that if their son was innocent of his crime and still alive, it would be as much of a miracle as the chicken on his plate still being alive. In that instant the roasted bird stood up and crowed.

For hundreds of years there have been two white chickens kept in an ornate cage-like recess inside the cathedral to commemorate that "miracle." Not the same birds, of course, but a continuous revolving display of two chickens that are clearly well fed and tended. I laughed when I heard the sound of chickens crowing inside the church as I opened the door to visit. Later I learned it's good luck to hear the crowing as it is as well to find one of their feathers on the floor of the sanctuary.

After looking at the treasures in the church, including the tomb of Saint Dominic, I lighted another candle for Grace and went on to the museum connected to the cathedral. There were a number of beautiful polychrome figures of saints in the collection. The carved wooden figures were by far my favorite art form on the Camino to that point. Their style was Gothic with some remaining bit of the Byzantine about them. The colors of the painted figures glowed with the richness of the pigments used. I stopped to do some drawings of two of my favorites and made notes about their colors, thinking I would do a little research on Spanish Gothic polychrome wooden figures when I got home.

An hour or more had passed and I was feeling cold. I wandered out of the coolness of the buildings to sit in the sun in a nearby plaza. I was writing in my journal and finishing up some of my drawings when a familiar voice interrupted me.

"'El-lo, my friend!" a voice exclaimed. "You okay, no?"

I looked up to see Diana from Quebec. I jumped up and put my arms around her and laughed with excitement at seeing her again. We rocked back and forth together, both sensing the pleasure of seeing a familiar face. Although I hadn't given up hope of finding her again, I thought she had probably moved on since I saw her from my window two days before.

"Yes, yes, *oui, oui*—I'm more than 'okay.' I'm doing just fine! Getting stronger and stronger. Look, my knees are normal again." Lifting my pant legs, I displayed the no-longer-swollen joints.

"*Bon, bon!*" she beamed.

"I have your money, too!" Reaching into my money pack that I wore around my neck and kept tucked into my shirt, I drew out the bills I owed her.

"Really, I can't tell you how much I appreciate your generosity in lending me the money. Thank you from the bottom of my heart. You didn't even know if I'd ever pay you back, or if we'd even ever see each other again." I was going on and on. "Bah—*merci, merci beaucoup!*"

It was clear that she hadn't understood all that I had fired at her but she smiled and responded simply with, "Is okay. Is nothing," as she reached out to take the money and shove it into her pants pocket.

We sat together on the steps in our now familiar quiet way. Diana began to eat some lunch she had brought to the plaza and offered me some cheese. With a little effort, I learned that she too had decided to stay a few days to rest in Santo Domingo before moving on. The night before she had stayed in a small hostel but it was expensive for her. I suggested the *hospitaleria* that the nuns ran where I was staying and she agreed to walk back with me to see if they had a room for her. Since I had decided to move on the next day, she could certainly have my room after I checked out. Whatever her decision was, I would never know. We said good-bye again in the lobby of the convent and I went up in the elevator for another nap, as she turned to speak to the woman behind the desk.

Later that afternoon I ventured out once more, this time to go to the main post office. I had the idea of carefully reviewing everything in my backpack and gathering up anything I could find that I really didn't need or wasn't using. My plan was to make a package to send to myself *poste restante* (similar to the U.S. general delivery) in Santiago where I could pick it up when I got there. I sent letters to my son *poste restante* when he was traveling in India and thought it might just work for me too. By sending things ahead, I could lighten my load a little and maybe make the remaining miles a little easier.

My drawing pad, several drawing pencils, brushes and watercolors weren't being used. (I never felt that I could sit and spend enough time on a watercolor—preferring to make drawings in my journal.) I put aside my swimming suit (where and when was I going to go bathing?); a wrap for cool evenings (I was always asleep before sunset and never experienced a "cool evening"); and quite a number of tourist brochures I had picked up along the way. It didn't seem like much but I was delighted to find, when the postal worker weighed it, the package came to 2.5 kilos—just about five pounds!

My next task was to find out what time the bus to Burgos left the following morning and to look for the precise place in the nearby plaza where I would board it. Since I only knew a very few Spanish words, and couldn't find anyone to tell me about the bus schedule in English, I was anxious about possibly mixing up directions and instructions so I practiced the where and when of my departure that afternoon before returning to my room for yet another nap.

The next morning would be the second time on the walk that my rain poncho was needed. I hadn't had to pull it out of my pack since the climb up the *Sierra del Perdón* outside of Pamplona—except to wonder if I should put it in the package I sent *poste restante* the day before. Luckily, I concluded that there just might be a day when I'd need it—and this was that day. Looking from the small window in my room, I could see the gray, rain-soaked skies and the heavy drizzle that was falling.

There were stretches
of road ... where the
Camino ...
followe...
alongside ...
road and occasionally
I saw ahead of me
a single
pilgrim

The weight of my backpack seemed a little more manageable as I once again hooked my arms into the straps and belted it around my waist. I couldn't decide if that was because of my having had such a good rest or if the five pounds I sent on to Santiago really made that much difference. Clearly the backpack belt cinched-in tighter than it had, a good sign that my own weight had gone down some—probably at least five pounds, maybe even more.

The night before, I had gotten excited about finding other ways to cut back on the weight I'd be carrying. I left behind some skin lotion— I would rely on my sunblock as a moisturizer and I poured out half of the shampoo and conditioner I had in two travel bottles. I could buy more as I needed it. Along with squeezing out most of the large tube of toothpaste I had (better to have brought a small tube and just replaced it as I needed it), I broke my comb in half, threw away some pages from a sketch pad I had decided to keep with me and left a neck scarf behind that I should have put in the post. Could I possibly have disposed of still one more pound?

I stood in the shelter of the bus pavilion in the plaza holding in my hand what I hoped was the correct amount of money for the fare. Several other people, including pilgrims, gathered around me to escape the now pouring rain. The group of us waited sullenly, shivering in the cool morning air and glancing up occasionally to see if the bus was approaching. When it did arrive, I was the first to get on and I felt my spirits lift as I scanned the faces of the other passengers, and saw other pilgrims, including The Irish Priest.

"Good morning, Father!" I greeted, "I'm so happy to see you again! I'd heard that you had stopped walking and no one could tell me what became of you!"

"Oh, deary me," he replied in his lilting brogue, "Well, I'm jus' fine, thank yooo! Noooo-o-o-o, I ne'er planned ta walk the whole thing ma' dear, oh no! I'm in terrible shape to doo such walkin'! I wanted ta jus get a wee taste of it in the beginnin' and then hoop the booses and trains along the way. I walked ta' Logroño, ya know," he said proudly, "then I hooped the boos. I've been stoppin' har and thar for some visits, otherwise I'da been doone ba' now."

"And, what aboot yoo? How's it been goin' along the way for yoo on yur 'mission,' hey?"

I told the Priest about my decision to stop and rest in Santo Domingo after my knees had gotten so swollen and that I planned to move on just as far as Burgos that day. Then I'd see how I felt when I got there. I hadn't given up on getting to Santiago, one way or the other, and most importantly, I wanted to get Grace's ashes to the *Cruz de Ferro*. If I felt I couldn't go on after that, I'd head back to Madrid and home.

"Oh, I've a feelin' yoo'll be makin' the *Cruz de Ferro*, for sure, ma' dear! And when you doo, yoo'll be settin' down yur burden thar. Yoo'll fly with the wings of an angel, awll the way ta Santiago! Yes, indeed."

His words brought tears to my eyes. I suppose the encouragement was what I had hoped for, but the lightness I felt was indescribable. I turned in the seat I had taken in front of him and smiled with an immense sense of knowing that I would make it. Having slipped my pack off under my poncho, I sat clutching it on my lap and breathed a sigh of relief. I no longer felt ashamed about having to ride the bus to Burgos. Many other pilgrims had obviously decided not to walk in the rain and continued to mount the bus as we drove along the rain-swept highway. It was going to be just fine, I told myself. *All is well.*

Clearly the day had put a crimp in the style of The Dutch Couple Who Picnic's plans, too. They got on the bus at Belgrado, a short distance from Santo Domingo. They were dripping wet in their rain ponchos. We smiled and nodded to one another as they took a seat across from mine.

"Glad to see you're able to move on," said the Dutchman. "Good for you! Not much of a day for walking though, is it?" He took off his rain hat and let the water drip from it into the aisle between us.

"Yes, thank you. I'm feeling much better. I wanted to move on since I've lost a few days on my schedule. I'll see how I feel after a day in Burgos."

With that, we fell silent and I sat watching the soaking countryside from the window next to me as the bus moved steadily on. There were stretches of roadway where the Camino followed alongside the road and occasionally I saw a small group or a single pilgrim walking purposefully in the drenching rain. Some interesting chapels and shrines appeared and quickly faded past. The rhythmic thumping of the bus's windshield wipers sounded like the beating heart of us all—moving on down the road—to whatever came next.

As I watched the landscape pass quickly by, my thoughts drifted back over the years I had spent with Grace. Whispy images of the incidences and decisions that brought me to this journey began to come together in my mind.

Sometimes the slightest shift in the
way you look at things, a seemingly insignificant
change in perspective, can alter your life forever.

Author Unknown

"Good, Reen, her apartment stinks like hell!"

Frank was calling from Pittsburgh where he had just arrived to pack up Grace and drive a truck with her things to Boston where I was living.

She was eighty years old and had been living alone in a one-bedroom subsidized apartment in downtown Pittsburgh. She had moved there not long after my father died, more than thirty years before. He had left her some money but within a few years she'd gone through it all. The small Social Security check she received monthly was her only income.

Grace's minimal housekeeping habits and lack of personal hygiene had deteriorated with her age. Her apartment had become a clutter of stained and dirty furniture, old boxes of craft supplies she kept herself busy with, and unwashed laundry. Food was caked on kitchen surfaces and pots were put back in cabinets without being washed. She was becoming more and more reclusive and when she did go out, she might easily have been taken for a homeless person in her stained and threadbare clothing. Her difficulty with speech had escalated, her eyesight was slowly fading into macular degeneration and she had undiagnosed diabetes—all of which made her vulnerable.

My brother and I had agreed that it would be a good idea for Grace to be within reach of one of us to check in on her from time to time. He had been living in Santa Barbara for many years and I was in Boston then so it became an "eenie-meenie" kind of decision as to which coast Grace would migrate to. She didn't seem to have a preference.

Since we had both left home as teenagers, neither of us had visited her more than once every year or two—with an obligatory phone call at Christmas, Thanksgiving, and Easter. It was difficult for me to be around her for more than short periods of time, even in her old age. Too much that had been left unsaid; too much that was hidden. Her anger and irritability were still her most common fallback emotional responses to just about anything that crossed her path, and, even with that, she tried too hard to please us and keep us entertained when we did visit. Consequently, visits were tense and uncomfortable. We had very little in common with her any longer, except of course, our history. Her many angry decrees while we were growing-up, that her life would have been better if she hadn't had any children, left her a very lonely woman.

To her credit, Grace developed a community of friends and a pattern of life that she was comfortable with. She taught classes in beading—necklaces, earrings, and Christmas ornaments—to a group of ladies at the YWCA in downtown Pittsburgh and she attended exercise classes there. She complained bitterly about how "stupid" her students were but continued to punish herself with them for over twenty years. Occasionally she swam in the pool at the Center and enjoyed walking the few blocks up Fifth Avenue to have lunch in the dining room of Kaufmann's Department Store.

All of these daily fixtures in her life would change abruptly with her move but it was a move that she was, at the time, anxious to make. By some default of fate, which I no longer remember, Grace would arrive by plane at Logan Airport and her boxes of clutter and dirty clothes would be driven by Frank, in a rented truck, to the apartment I had found for her. She would, of course, not like the apartment and find any number of things wrong with my choice but I had come to expect that and braced myself to try to make the best of it.

Over the next five years, she moved three more times. There was always something about each apartment that was not quite right. It was either the size of the rooms, the fact that there was no view, the lack of bus service, unavailable or unacceptable shopping opportunities, and the other people in the building. Her issues with the housing I found for her was a repeat of a pattern she had cultivated during the years my brother and I were growing up. Consequently, he and I had to adjust to a new school and make new friends eleven times before we got to high school. We learned to be each other's best friend. When asked, I'd explain that we were moving again because my mother didn't like her kitchen. My father, of course, just complied to keep the peace. His example was probably what prompted me to find her still another place to live. I continued trying to be the perfect daughter—hoping she'd find some happiness and possibly see in me something she appreciated.

Eventually, after discovering her lying on the floor a couple of times, unable to get up, I resorted to looking for in-home care. That was a very undependable arrangement that turned out to be a little sketchy (*Did that woman really take some money in the drawer or was it just misplaced?*) and ultimately, a complete botch. I had to end the whole thing when I learned that one woman was giving Grace her dinner at three in the afternoon just so she could get home to her family by their usual dinner hour. Finally I searched for a nursing home where she would be looked after. I was getting more and more exhausted trying to help her keep her independence. It was a decision I was trying to avoid but one that had to be made. The disappointment I felt was visceral and definitely added to my sense of guilt and my sympathy for her.

Her last years were not easy on either one of us. They drained her of any remaining interest in carrying on and she told me, on an almost daily basis, how much she'd like to end it. Sometime during her last year, when she was living in a home outside of Washington, D.C. where I had moved her again, she asked me to help her die but recognized immediately the impossibility of that. Even if I'd known what to do to help her, I would be incapable of carrying out the task.

After a little more than an hour, the bus pulled into the *Plaza de Vega* on the southern side of the *Rio Arlanzon,* which dissects Burgos. The forty-five miles, that would have taken me at least three days to walk, went by quickly. Burgos, at one time the capitol of the United Kingdom of Castile and León looked prosperous. Traffic bustled with late-model French, American and Japanese cars. The people were well dressed and walked purposefully to wherever they were headed. Lace-like spires of the beautiful Gothic cathedral soared above the buildings on the other side of the river.

The passengers on the bus began to rise from their seats in their still-wet clothes and rain gear. The air was musty and humid as we shuffled slowly toward the exit. The rain had stopped though the sky was still heavy with the threat of more to come. The Irish Priest followed me down the steps of the bus and I turned to ask him where he planned to stay in Burgos.

"Well, I dunno. I suspect I shoold be able ta get somethin' hereaboots," he responded as he gestured with his arm to indicate the plaza where we stood.

"Well, would you mind if I tag along?" I asked. "I need to get a room too and I haven't a clue where to start. With your Spanish, could you ask for a room for me too?"

He agreed and said he'd be doing it "on the cheap," looking for a room in a *pensión*, and I agreed that would be fine with me and my budget. Conditions accepted, we started walking around the plaza and the adjacent streets looking for signs for rooms. The first *pensión* we stopped at was up a flight of dirty steps and not very appealing— with chipped paint and graffiti covered walls and a concierge who looked drunk. No, thank you. I thought. After stopping at a few even more seedy looking places and finding that none of them had a vacancy, we went full circle and decided on the hotel that was right next to the bus station. Not exactly a "budget" place but it looked clean and safe.

Again there was an embarrassing moment, as there had been at Roncesvalles, when the man at the desk assumed that The Irish Priest and I were a couple. We each got our separate keys, however, and went our separate ways. I felt the priest had not enjoyed the responsibility of helping me find a room and would probably have taken one of the rooms in the very first place we looked if I hadn't been with him— drunken concierge and all.

I located my room and slipped out of my poncho, unsnapped the belt of my backpack, and rested it on the floor next to the bed. It definitely did feel lighter and I was thrilled to think that it actually might be possible to carry it more easily. My spirits were up and I wanted to look around Burgos.

The stunning Gothic cathedral across the river is the third largest in Spain—the largest is in Seville and the second largest, Toledo. Walking out of the hotel to cross the river on the *Puente Santa Maria*, I headed straight for the church.

On both sides of the river there are stretches of park-like greens with large shade trees and willows reaching over the stonewall embankments down to the slow moving river below. Cafes line the promenades that edge the streets that follow the course of the river. It was almost a pastoral scene, more like the setting you'd see in a small town than in a bustling city of over 150,000.

Grace would have liked to see this beautiful place from her wheelchair. There weren't any sea gulls to feed, of course, but she'd be fascinated by the variety of buildings, how the people dressed, and the food was displayed in the windows. In the last months of her life, there had been a shift in her way of dealing with the world. She wasn't angry anymore and had become less fearful. She admired things we passed on our weekly outings—a beautiful tree, some flowers blooming in a garden, a sweet puppy.

The French Gothic influences in the architectural style of the *Catedral de Burgos* (or *Catedral de Santa Maria*) was evident even from a distance as I looked up at the twin spires with their tracery and open work. Antonio Gaudí, the 20th century Spanish architect of organic and soaring lines surely would have found inspiration here for his *Sagrada Familia* in Barcelona. The interior layout of the church was a jumble, however, with many chapels and additional buildings, the cloister, and still more chapels added around the apse and adjoining the central nave. Begun in the early 13th century, with construction lasting over 500 years, the building is positioned on a sloping hillside. One major doorway toward the north is at a different level than another, facing it in the south wall.

Scaffolding was set-up inside and out of the massive building. The stone was being cleaned and the contrast between the cleaned and not-yet-cleaned stone was startling. Gleaming white limestone that was revealed beneath years of accumulated gray added light and grandeur to the interior space. The cleaned exterior stone gave the illusion of the building floating skyward.

There was an enormous collection of gilded and polychrome figures and architectural treasures throughout the public areas. Incredibly beautiful alters and intricately carved wooden choir stalls—as well as stone sculptures of saints and framed Baroque Italianesque paintings were in evidence everywhere I looked. Several royal families of Castile and León were buried in ornately carved

stone sarcophagi and placed in their respective family's gilded chapels. The Spanish freedom fighter and national hero, Rodrigo Diaz de Vivar, known as *El Cid*, was born five miles north of Burgos in the 11th century, and in 1919 was interred, with his wife Jimena, in the cathedral. A large rose-colored marble slab, inscribed with their names is cordoned off with ropes just outside of the choir stall. There's also a particularly magnificent grille that separates a large chapel (*Capilla del Condestable*) from the rest of the cathedral. It has beautifully worked intricacies of wood that look impossibly like lace. Not surprisingly, UNESCO has listed the Burgos Cathedral as a World Heritage Site for its masterful Spanish Gothic style.

As I wandered around the vast space, it was easy to pick out other pilgrims from the general crowd. With the telltale backpacks and sometimes the scallop shell worn around the neck or pinned to a backpack, pilgrims did stand out. It was just familiar faces I greeted there that day, though. I had none of the "identifiers." My backpack was at the hotel and I didn't have a guidebook with me. The loose sheets I'd been using as my guide probably got lost in my hurry to catch the bus in Santo Domingo. Although tempted, I decided not to replace them with a book and add to the weight of the pack again.

Leaving by one of the huge, carved side doors, I wandered up the hill behind the cathedral toward a park where the remains of an old castle stood. Three separate wedding parties were vying for the "best" locations to have their wedding pictures taken to record their important day. Intermittent drizzle kept interrupting their photo sessions and brides, grooms and ladies in colorful gowns were frequently scattering all around the park to find shelter.

Further along at the top of the hill was an awe-inspiring panorama of the city below. A long, curving cast bronze sort of map stands at waist height at the edge of the pathway and serves as a guide to the scene in the distance.

It was beginning to rain in earnest again. I turned from the misty view and quickly headed downhill to a tented cafe at the foot of a long flight of steps next to the cathedral. I settled into a chair at a table that was pushed up to one of the large clear plastic windows that ran all around the tent. Even with the rain hitting the window heavily now, I could see people dashing by in the plaza, trying to avoid getting wet. The cafe was nearly empty—a little late for lunch and far too early for a Spaniard to have dinner. I hadn't eaten all day so I was ravenous. I ordered red peppers stuffed with codfish, a green salad, crusty bread and a glass of regional white wine.

The Dutch Couple Who Picnic suddenly burst into the shelter of the tent and shook off the rain from their ponchos like two wet dogs. I hailed them and asked them to join me for a drink. They were ending their walk in Burgos and heading back home on an overnight train to Paris, then on to Rotterdam in the morning. Their names were Laney and Pete. Laney felt more at ease with me by then and actually spoke English very well. We chatted for an hour or so while we waited for the rain to stop. It was always easy to sit with fellow pilgrims and feel comfortable even when there was very little common language or when there were periods of silence in the conversation. Maybe it was the power of the shared experience that offered that mutual sense of comfort.

We all looked out the plastic window at once at the sound of yelling and laughing coming down the street opposite the cafe. The clamor was The Mexican Boy Scouts riding by the tent on bicycles at break neck speed. They were whooping and yelling with the fun of riding fast through the rain. I wondered out-loud where they'd gotten the bikes.

Pete explained, "Yes, Marco told me that they had actually bought them in Madrid when they first arrived and had them shipped to Burgos. They arranged to pick them up here and ride the bikes the rest of the way to Santiago. Good planning on their part, I must say!"

"Oh, actually, they have some relatives—family—in Madrid who helped with the shipping," Laney added.

While my single day as a tourist in Burgos had been interesting, I decided I didn't want to stay on there, after all. It would take a week to see all the art treasures in the cathedral alone, and many days to wander around the rest of the city. I longed for the sense of adventure I had when I'd been walking as a true pilgrim, however, and wanted to ignite that feeling in myself again. Laney and Pete encouraged me to go by train to León across the high, wind swept plateau of the western part of the province of Castile. The *meseta*, as it's called, is very desolate, barren, and flat. Two other pilgrims I spoke with in Santo Domingo said that if I had to ride through any of the Camino, the *meseta* was the best part to miss.

The rain was ending. The sun was beginning to shine on the plaza and reflect in the droplets that ran down the plastic windows. I wanted to get to the train station to buy a ticket to León on an early train before the rain started again. With Laney and Pete's directions and a small map Pete drew for me on a paper napkin, I said my final "good-bye"s to them and headed out of the tent. *"Buen Camino!"* I waved as I looked back and turned to duck out of the shelter.

At the station I bought a ticket for a noon departure for León the following day and walked back to my room for another nap.

When we are sure that we are on the right road
there is no need to plan our journey too far ahead.
No need to burden ourselves with doubts and fears
as to the obstacles that may bar our progress.
We cannot take more than one step at a time.

Orison Swett Marden

Looking from the window of the train, I could see the *meseta* rolling on in every direction. At the height of the Camino's popularity, early writers describe an unending line of pilgrims on this great Castilian plateau, walking in front and behind far out to the horizon in both directions. By contrast, at the times when the train and the Camino came into proximity, I saw only occasional groups of pilgrims trudging along in the growing heat of the day. There were herds of sheep grazing as herds had in the Middle Ages. Burgos had been a center for a variety of commerce that centered on wool—buying, trading, washing, carding, spinning, dying and weaving. The wool from the sheep of the *meseta* was the fodder for the medieval prosperity of Burgos.

There had actually been many more pilgrims at the train station in Burgos when I arrived that morning, than I saw on the trail in the distance, however. At the station I greeted some of those I had passed along the way and learned that they were taking the train on to Santiago de Compostela or at least to a city further along—Astorga, Ponferrada, or the modern city of Sarria, which would leave them with only a few days walk to Santiago. The distance to Santiago from León was less than 200 miles and the train would take the pilgrims there in six hours time. I didn't want to think about how long it would take me to walk there. I was certain that I wanted to get back on the Camino again and keep walking as long as I could. The best estimate I could make, without my "guidebook" sheets, was that León was about fifty miles from the *Cruz de Ferro*. *I know I can make it that far*, I thought.

Some other pilgrims, though, were simply ending their walk and going in the opposite direction toward "home." The French trio, the *Ménage á Trois*, was sitting on a bench sipping steaming cups of coffee. The two sisters giggled and waved from a distance as I walked toward them to say hello. I gathered, through sign language and something that felt like a game of charades, they were going back to Toulouse. Actually, I had heard they had left the walk already but it seemed much too complicated to question why they had continued to Burgos.

Several groups of pilgrims were hurrying about the station looking for the platform for their departing trains. The sound of a voice from a loudspeaker rapidly firing out announcements of trains coming and trains leaving filled the atmosphere with a sense of urgency. Several pilgrims were sitting on the floor near a wall, resting against their backpacks or leaning on their walking sticks. Two or three looked like they might have been waiting for the train since the early morning hours. All but a few looked haggard, worn-out, and disheveled. The Irish Priest arrived just minutes before the train to Santiago pulled out of the station and I saw from my window seat that he got on just in time. As the train rolled out of the station and on through the outskirts of the city, I walked back to where he was sitting to talk with him for what would probably be one last time.

He was breathless as he sat wiping his brow with his handkerchief. "Whew, thought I woodn't make it! Started out early ba' jus' got distracted. Burgos is sooch a pretty city, heh?"

We talked for a few minutes about what we each had done in Burgos as the train slowly eased out of the station and through the outlying areas. As it picked-up speed, we shook hands and I said good-bye to him.

"Fly with tha' wings you've groon, ma' dear!" he waved and called out as I walked back to my seat. "Fly with wings! *Buen Camino!*"

His words embarrassed me. They made me sound virtuous in a way I certainly didn't feel I was. Usually when people heard that I was carrying my mother's ashes, they would look at me reverently and marvel at what a good person I must be or what a wonderful woman my mother must have been.

Oh, If they only knew! I'd think. I simply wanted to do this thing I had set out to do. When I started on the journey, there were far too many reasons "why" to say for sure what my primary motivation for bringing her ashes was. It was certainly complex and mixed with issues like finally saying good-bye as much as relief that she had gone and sadness for her unhappy life and wanting so much to just give up the whole thing. Give up my sense of responsibility for her; my identity with my grievances about her—not the least of which was giving her a place that I could be proud of. It was *my* pride. I didn't want to think of my mother as just being tossed in the ocean somewhere.

After arriving at the train station in León, I had expected to see many other pilgrims getting off the train with me and I assumed I'd just follow in the direction they were walking and eventually arrive at the Camino or find signs to a *refugio*.

There were, as it happened, only a couple of people that I could distinguish as pilgrims who got off at León and they walked out of the station in as questioning a way as I did. No obvious signs that I noticed pointed the way to the Camino from the station—no shells, no yellow arrows, not even a municipal sign that just spelled it out. I decided not to follow the others who seemed confused too. Instead, I headed in the opposite direction toward what looked like a major plaza and city center.

Two women seated on a bench in the sun watched me as I crossed the wide plaza that faced a gleaming, palatial, white stone building. A sign near the building's entrance read *"Convento de San Marcos."* The facade of the majestic building is another beautiful example of the Plateresque style, which, in Spain, bridged the Gothic and the Renaissance styles of Spanish architecture. The building was begun in the late 12th century and acquired its ornate facade 400 years later. Originally it was a hospital and refuge for pilgrims on their way to Santiago and was later used as a monastery for the military monks of the Order of Santiago. Its other many uses included, civilian prison, church, army barracks, and horse stable, before it was restored and elegantly furnished for its most recent incarnation as one of the luxury hotels, *paradors,* that the government now owned.

"Excuse me," the dark-haired woman called out. "Are you American?"

"Yes, I am." I responded with a smile. It was clear by her English that she was, too.

"Are you walking the Camino, then?" she continued in a slight lilting way that was maybe the result of living in England or Australia for a while.

I nodded, smiled, and repeated, "Yes, I am."

We introduced ourselves and she and her friend explained that they had gone to college together. The woman who initially greeted me, Jan, had just finished a job in England and had been traveling for a couple of months. The woman who did very little talking was living in Rome with her husband and two small children. The two had decided to have a reunion in León for a few days of sight seeing.

I unbuckled the belt of my backpack, slipped my arms out of the straps and lowered it down onto the end of the bench they were sharing. Stretching my shoulder blades back and arching my back, I breathed a sigh of relief from the return of the weight and asked if I could join them on the bench.

"I've been thinking about doin' it myself, but, I dunno'. I thought I could just start from here and try to walk it—or at least some of it. How're you liking it?" Jan asked. Her travels of the last months were clearly not yet over.

I laughed in response, "Well, it's been an amazing adventure but I wouldn't say I was necessarily 'liking' it!"

I didn't want to discourage an adventure she had in mind so I avoided describing the difficulties of my last few days and decided to emphasize how important it was to plan.

"You have to have enough water with you and enough food to keep up your energy. You don't want to carry very much weight with you, so you should know what the distances are between towns and villages so you can plan to buy food or have a meal in a bar or someplace like that," I cautioned. "If you can get by without very much weight in your pack, it will be a hundred times easier. Just a couple of pounds can make all the difference!"

We talked about some of the essentials she'd need if she decided to walk even a small part of the Camino. She had some good walking shoes she pointed out as she lifted her feet straight out in front of her. She'd need a bigger backpack than the one she had been traveling with and, maybe she could get by without a sleeping bag since I mentioned that many of the *refugios* offer blankets. I told her I had never been willing to sleep with one of those communal blankets over me, but she didn't seem to be as squeamish as I was.

143

After chatting with the two friends for a while, I felt the need to move on and stood up to put my pack on again signaling the end of our conversation. Like a homing pigeon I was focused on finding the Camino and getting "officially" back on the Walk.

Looking off over my shoulder toward the buildings in the near distance, I said, "Well, I'd better get going. Do you know where the Camino is? Did you see any markers over there?" I gestured to the right with my head.

Jan wagged a finger toward a busy intersection that bordered the plaza, "There were some of those shell-kinda' signs there. Maybe that's the way to the Camino? Maybe someone can tell you where there's a *refugio* though, I really don't know about that. You're gonna' stay here tonight then? Or, I dunno,' maybe you're just gonna' start walking again?" she asked, clearly interested in my plans.

"Yeah, I think I'll find the *refugio* now and look around León this afternoon. I'd rather get a fresh start on the Walk in the morning," I explained.

We said our good-byes and I left them sitting on the bench with an encouraging word for Jan to try to walk some of the Camino.

"I'm sure you'll meet lots of interesting people and, if you don't like walking, you can always just quit," I offered. *Who was I to be so cavalier— that sentiment certainly didn't seem to apply to me.* With a wave to them both, I walked across the plaza in the direction Jan had indicated, crossed the street that bordered it, and began looking for Camino markers.

Once I spotted one marker, the others were easier to locate. They were bronze and some looked quite old. I learned later that many of the shell markers throughout León's medieval quarter were, in fact, very old but no one could tell me just how long they had been pointing pilgrims in the right direction. Unlike all the days before, I was walking east, rather than west. The center of the old quarter was east of the plaza where I had stopped. If I had walked west, I would have soon found myself on the road that crosses the *Rio Bernesga* and out once again into the *meseta* that surrounds all of León on that great plateau.

Walking through the more modern city with its straight streets and grid-like plan I crossed the wide *Plaza de Santo Domingo* and entered the medieval quarter. Once there, I continued to follow the Camino signs "backwards" until I stumbled on a *refugio* that was part of a Benedictine convent, *Las Madres Carvajal*. This was the very one, of the two *refugio*s I was told were in León, that I had hoped to find. The nuns in the convent were known as *Benedictinas* and they had an evening service in the small chapel through a door just next to the door leading to the *refugio*. With a name like *Benedictinas*, I smiled and wondered if they sang with accompanying castanets.

I signed the guest book and paid the fee at the reception table near the entrance that was attended by a young woman who smiled warmly and said *"Hola!"* I thought I'd have to explain the days in my passport that did not carry a stamp since the last one I got was in Santo Domingo. The young woman, however, thought little of what I was trying to say and just stamped my book and waved me past her and into the hallway that lead to the sleeping rooms.

The interior of the *refugio* itself was divided into men's and women's sleeping and showering areas much like the one in Azofar but even more strictly defined. I counted my blessings as I made my way past the smelly boots lined-up outside the men's quarters. Opening an unmarked stippled glass and metal door, I looked into a room that served as a small kitchen. Several young men and women were sitting around a table that was pushed up against the far wall. They were sharing a bottle of wine and all talking and laughing at the same time in a northern language I couldn't identify. Looking up at me they said in unison, *"Hola, señora! Buen Camino!"* and raised their glasses toward me. I returned the greeting with a smile and let the door slowly close on their celebration. The salute they gave me was a wonderful welcoming to my being back on the Camino.

Since I hadn't arrived soaked in sweat and tired from a day's walk, I decided against taking advantage of the showers and simply chose a bunkbed, dug out my sleeping bag, slid my backpack under the bunk and laid down to take a nap. An afternoon's rest had become a welcome and delicious part of my day at that point. Indeed, as I lay there in the quiet, darkened room, I began to think of how I might incorporate a nap into my daily routine once I got back home. Even a short, seated rest would be a lovely way to get some of the benefits of a full out *"siesta."*

After only a few minutes my peaceful thoughts were interrupted when a short, barrel-chested, bearded man burst into the room to describe to his followers, in full voice Spanish, something or other about the room and, I can only imagine, the importance of quickly grabbing a good bed. I surprised myself by partially sitting up in my bunk, glaring at the group and *shush*ing the intruder, before turning over and pulling my sleeping bag up over my head. Fortunately he quieted down and the

group of five or six left the women's room allowing the door behind them to slam. Several sleepy women around me called out expletives in a variety of languages.

Sleep wouldn't come, so with a sigh, I swung my feet out of the bunk to put my boots back on and go out to look around León.

With no particular destination in mind, I started off to the north of the convent in the direction of the cathedral whose towers I glimpsed as I ambled through the winding streets. The winds were picking up and the temperature was suddenly much colder. I hadn't felt so cold since leaving the Pyrenees. The Cantabrian Mountains lie to the north of León and can bring on strong cold winds even in the summer. I huddled in my zip-up windbreaker, stuffed my hands into the pockets and picked up my pace, seeking out the sunny side of the narrow streets at every turn.

The open plaza where the *Santa Maria de la Regia Catedral* stood was crowded with groups of young people huddled together on the steps surrounding the stunning early Gothic building. They were pouring over their guidebooks, sitting close together to stay warm. A group of tourists were standing in a circle, listening to their guide who was speaking another language I didn't recognize—could it be Portuguese? He was holding on to his hat with one hand, pointing toward a stained glass window with the other. Many other people—pilgrims, tourists, and locals were sitting in the sun and well out of the wind. Two small children were jumping up and down the steps in unison, holding hands, while their mothers leaned back leisurely into the sun and talked quietly, not seeming to notice the chill.

What I assumed was the main door to the church was closed and locked, as were all the other doors I tried as I walked around all sides of the massive structure. The two towers that flanked either side of the triple doorways on the west side were of different heights and had obviously not been built with an eye to symmetry. Or, since several different architects designed the cathedral over the 200 years that it was under construction, they are likely towers from different centuries. Wonderful carvings were at the center one of the three doors. The shear number and height of the stained-glass windows that were almost side-by-side in every exterior wall amazed me. I could only imagine the quality of the interior light, infused with the soft colors of the remarkable windows. There was an enormous rose window high above the west doors and another over the south entrance as well, both of which I wasn't going to be able to see from the inside.

Disappointed that once again my timing wasn't going to gain me entrance to a building I had wanted to see, I decided to just go for a walk around the city. I turned and headed across the plaza in the direction of modern León.

As I strolled passed stylish shops and store fronts, my heavy boots, crumpled cotton pants and windbreaker looked even shabbier compared to all the stylishly dressed Leónese. Seeing myself reflected in a store window, I swiped at my hair in an attempt to smooth down the strays and stood more erect as I walked along. The good-looking people of León filled the sidewalks as they either went about shopping or huddled together against the wind in the cafes that lined the streets. The women wore their hair stylishly—trimmed and kempt—and had slim figures. In fact, the men and even the young people all seemed well dressed and prosperous. Unlike the more casual style we Americans have taken on, the women of León, for the most part, wore skirts and tailored suits with fashionable shoes—no running shoes here! Grown children held hands as they walked along with adults. Family groups enjoyed chance meetings with friends. Even the traffic noises added to the upbeat atmosphere.

After an hour of walking around, the cold wind that cut through my thin jacket was making me very uncomfortable and I was getting hungry. When I turned to cross the street and head back into the medieval quarter, I spotted a quick sandwich place, modeled on our American Subway chain. I picked out a *"Mediterraneo"* (it was tuna) from the photograph displayed on the wall menu and ordered a *cervesa* (beer) with two chocolate cookies to go. Carrying my dinner with me, I made my way back to the *refugio* in time to eat and go to the *Benedictina*'s pilgrim service

I took a seat in one of the few rows of benches in the small chapel that was next to the *refugio*. I could just make out the cloistered nuns at the front of the room filing in to take their places behind a wooden openwork screen that protected them from any interaction with the outside world. The group of fifteen or so walked in single file, with heads bowed and in silence. Another woman, who looked to be a layperson, stood up in front of the altar, greeted us, and spoke a few words. When she was finished, she stepped down to take a seat at the side of the dimly lit room and the service began.

The Pilgrim's Service consisted entirely of the beautiful singing by the nuns behind the grille. There was no translation necessary, as is often true with the universality of music. One singer in particular outshined all the others. The clear, bell tones of her soprano voice was so uplifting, it brought tears to my eyes. The songs the sweet sounding *Benedictinas* sang for us that evening, which sounded very much like the chant-like songs of the medieval nun, Hildegard of Bingen, were also very likely the same songs that had been sung to pilgrims for centuries.

After the service had already begun, The Gruppo Spañiardos, as I called them, the same ones who burst into the women's room at the *refugio*, all noisily took seats in the row in front of me. The leader talked in a stage whisper throughout the service and I nearly *shush*ed him again, but I resisted the urge. Several of the dozen or so other pilgrims turned and glared at him but he didn't seem to notice. He rattled on in Spanish, gesturing towards different areas of the chapel, spewing his wealth of information about the service, the chapel and who-knows-what else. He and his group showed up a few times along the path in the following days. I realized he was probably hired as a guide for the people he was with. Even though the group took advantage of the kitchens at the *refugios*, and attended pilgrim's services, I never saw them actually walking. Theirs was a "semi-pilgrim's" experience, most likely observed through the windows of an air-conditioned car.

The *refugio* had a gathering place just outside the entrance door and within a small courtyard area where pilgrims talked together, sitting on and leaning against the ancient walls of the building. Some reading material that related the history of the Camino (all in Spanish) was lying on a table, as well as a notebook where you could leave messages for other pilgrims, and a simple paper fold-out provided by the local group of supporters of the Camino, *Asociación de Amigos del Camino de Santiago de León.*

The black and white brochure was made up of four multi-columned tables that showed the names of all the towns, villages and cities between León and Santiago de Compostela—entries of about 150 places in total. It listed, in codes of C (*Comidas/bocadillo*—food / sandwich), T (*tienda comestibles*—a place to buy food), A (*albergue/refugio*—hotels or a *refugio*), and B (bar)—all of the essential information I was looking for. It also showed the distance each town was from the one before it and, in one panel of the three-fold sheet there was a drawing of the elevations of the walk from León to Ponferrada. In the days ahead, this simple brochure became as important a tool as my boots and backpack were to my walk. It took the place of a guidebook and I used it frequently throughout each day to calculate how far I had to walk to reach food, water and a bed for the night. If I had had something so complete and yet simple for the first part of my walk, it would have made all the difference in how I planned my days.

The next morning I awoke in a dark and quiet room. No sign of daylight came through the window at the head of my bunkbed. Only two other women were up and moving about with their flashlights flickering as they found their path through the labyrinth of beds. After a long, refreshing yawn and a very extended stretch, I swung my legs out of the bed, gathered up my towel and toothbrush and strode toward the toilets. The bright lights in the room made me squint as I made my way around several other women gathered at the sinks. No one made eye contact; there were no greetings—this was clearly not a social event. Back at my bunk, I rolled up my sleeping bag and repacked everything in the old familiar way, placing Grace low in the pack again. I mentally blew a kiss toward the black plastic box she had been traveling in and sighed, *Well, here we go again, Grace!*

I stowed the folded brochure in an outside pocket in my pants and once again, hoisted my backpack up and strapped the waistband around my much thinner waist. For the first time in days, I had a sense of "belonging" there. I felt lighter and stronger. My backpack was definitely lighter. I was rested and armed with much more information about where I was going and what I'd find ahead. Certainly the folded piece of paper that I patted in my pants pocket gave me more confidence but I also knew a great deal more about what the Camino was like in a way I couldn't possibly have known in my first days.

Through many dangers, toils and snares,
we have already come.
T'was Grace that brought us safe thus far,
and Grace will lead us home.

John Newton

The excitement I felt about getting on the Camino again was energizing and I surprised myself by stepping out of the *refugio* well before seven o'clock. Ambling through the quiet narrow streets of old León in the early morning light, I took a bite of the apple I bought the day before with the express purpose of having something to eat as I began my day. This time I wouldn't have to walk for two hours with nothing to eat before finding a bar open for coffee and breakfast.

The shell markers and yellow arrows weren't so obvious as I walked through the commercial streets of the city on my way out to the countryside. I was as confused as I'd been when I left the train station the day before. It was very important to stay observant. At least twice, I wandered down a street and had to backtrack to an intersection to check for Camino signs again.

After almost two hours, I had finally reached the outskirts of León. The city sprawled out and over some in-lying hills where cave-like houses were dug into the small rise in the ground. The doors that led into the dwellings, a chimney coming out at the top of the rise, and sometimes a single window was the extent of the grass-covered piles of earth that looked like someone's home. I watched intently to see if any gnomes might exit as I passed. I learned later that these cave-like dwellings

151

housed not little people but rather, wine. They're called *bodegas* and have been used for centuries to age and store wine. I wondered though if they might just as easily have housed people in some ancient past use.

On a stretch of a two-way street leading through a neighborhood of apartment buildings and shops, I could see two pilgrims, a man and a woman, walking on the sidewalk several blocks ahead of me. They had backpacks on and the woman had a walking stick that she held horizontally in one hand. Since the Camino markers were so few and far between, seeing the couple, I felt comforted that I was probably going in the right direction.

An old, bent woman entered a chapel on the other side of street. The small stone building was clearly very old, too. I dashed across the street quickly, dodging cars to read a plaque mounted next to the door. It mentioned the Camino de Santiago and something more—I couldn't make out the gist of it. The chapel had probably once been a considerable distance outside of León and maybe it had served as a kind of early stopping-off place for Leónese pilgrims setting out for Santiago. Now it appeared to be a suburban neighborhood church. I opened the heavy wooden door and quickly closed it. If I had entered, I felt I would have been intruding on what looked like a very private service. Candles on the altar dimly lit the small room. Only five people were kneeling forward with their hands clasped in prayer. A thin and frail looking white haired man with slumped shoulders was dressed in a long black garment. He stood facing the altar with his back to the room. His arms were raised as he spoke words I could barely hear.

Crossing the street again, I continued out of the city and looked up the hill ahead of me to see that the pilgrims I had noticed earlier were looking back toward me; looking away, then looking again. Finally, never slowing their pace the man looked back one more time and waved to me. After I returned the greeting, the woman waved too. It seemed a sweet gesture. I think it was meant to be reassuring for all of us that we were on the right path.

At Virgens del Camino I stopped for breakfast at a large restaurant at the top of a hill. The few other customers at the bar looked to be locals. They flashed a bored glance at me as I pushed open the heavy glass door and stood in the entrance and unbuckled my backpack. The news was on the television mounted on the wall behind the bar and music was coming from a radio somewhere in the large room.

I lowered my pack to the floor next to me and took a stool near the door. The menu, which was clearly printed for tourist, with photos of the dishes described, listed *platos de huevos*, egg dishes. It had been awhile since I had a Spanish omelette so my choice was obvious. The omelette with potatoes, when it arrived, had chopped fresh tomatoes on top and was served with warm, toasted, thick slices of crusty bread. A cluster of grapes garnished the plate. With two cups of my favorite *café con leché*, I was feeling very satisfied and happy to get moving on.

The first day back on the Camino was less than auspicious, however. There's an alternative Camino route I might have taken outside of León that was described by the overseer of the *refugio* the night before. She said it meanders across the countryside and passes through villages, and it's much more interesting than the more direct route. I, however, chose the direct route and therefore, had a grueling day of walking next to the highway. Cars and trucks were speeding past me on both sides of the two-lane road. I was covered in the dry, fine dirt kicked up by the traffic. There were no shade trees to rest under, no beautiful fields of flowers, no Roman ruins to be awed by or old chapels to admire. There were not even many pilgrims to greet— they had no doubt gone the other way. On several occasions along that stretch I thought of the proverbial "road not taken."

There were often options for the Camino, and this day of more than ten miles of highway walking—direct and to the destination— was a perfect example of how my choice affected the kind of day I had. Having taken the road less traveled by pilgrims, it did make all the difference.

By the time I reached the *refugio* at San Martín del Camino, I had walked fifteen miles and decided to stop for the night. I felt pretty good about having gone so far on my first day back on the walk. I wasn't particularly tired but I was filthy. Dirty grit had settled on every surface of my body, my clothes and my backpack. I longed for a shower and hoped the water at the *refugio* was at least warm, if not hot.

The building had probably been a school that had been converted to a *refugio* and run by the town. Many municipalities along the Camino find empty buildings to put to use for the benefit of the town as well as the pilgrims. There was a grass-covered area in front of the entrance with a table and some plastic chairs scattered about. As I entered the low, metal gate, there were other pilgrims sitting in the yard, some were resting against the building, reading, talking in groups, and some were hanging laundry on the low fence surrounding the outdoor space. Several people looked towards me and smiled or nodded and softly said, "*Hola.*"

I settled into my usual routine of choosing a bed, sliding my pack off and under the bed, and taking a shower. As the luke warm water washed away the days' grit and dust, I was completely refreshed and uplifted. I used the laundering routine I had established of standing on my clothes as I showered and then dressing in the clean clothes I'd brought with me into the shower room. Once dried and dressed, I went outside to hang the dripping laundry.

Chores completed, I looked up and down the entrance hall for someone to pay for the bed and for a stamp for my passport. There didn't seem to be an overseer there at the time but I did see a table at one end of the hall where there was a box for donations. I signed the registration book lying open on the table, stamped my passport in the usual way, and dropped the requisite euro coins into the box secured to the wall above the table.

The Gruppo Spañiardos were at the market across the highway where I had gone to buy something for dinner. They were, once again, all talking loud and keeping the shop owner busy with several demands. The leader pushed me aside as he reached for the apples I was about to select and, without so much as a, "*pardon me,*" he turned and added the fruit to the bags of groceries he was amassing on the counter. Later in the kitchen, I was trying to claim some of the table space, along with another young couple who had made their dinner earlier. The Gruppo took over what little available counter space there was, all of the cooking utensils and all of the drinking glasses lined-up on a shelf above the sink. The long kitchen table was all theirs for the grand meal they were preparing, except for the last couple of feet which the couple and I held on to.

Since there were no pots or pans available, it was a good thing that I'd planned a no-cook meal of a can of tuna fish and a tomato, some local cheese and a glass of wine. I was getting so irritated by my kitchen mates that I ate quickly and took my bottle of wine outside to escape, leaving the young couple to hold down their end of the table alone.

How I missed my friends from the first part of the walk—The Singing Señoritas, The Mexican Boy Scouts, Demetri from Brussels pedaling his bike and trailer to who-knows-where, The Dutch Couple

Who Picnic, Hanna and Horst, Diana from Quebec struggling along with her braces, The Irish Priest, even the jolly *Ménage á Trois*, but most of all, I missed The Architect.

Lamenting to myself, I thought, *If he were here now, everything would be different! It would be more fun! Even the Gruppo wouldn't seem so irritating. He'd start talking with people and soon we'd have friends all around us.*

Determined to do something to break out of my isolation and be friendlier myself, I followed what I thought would be The Architect's style: I approached a group of pilgrims sitting in the yard and offered them some of my wine.

"*Hola!* Sure! We'll have some wine!" replied a bearded, rosy-cheeked man sitting with a woman at a picnic table. He spoke with a heavy German accent. They both looked middle-aged and seemed to be thoroughly enjoying each other and this shared adventure. They laughed readily and touched each other often—an arm around the shoulder, a caress to the cheek.

He continued, "You're the woman we saw behind us coming up the hill out of León this morning!" He had most likely already been enjoying a glass or two of wine, judging from his slightly too jovial nature and his bloodshot eyes.

I opened a package of crackers I had gotten at the store and offered them to everyone. "Yes, yes, now I realize that was you! Well, I'm glad we all made it!" I replied as I reached across the table and poured them both some wine. A few others were sitting nearby and two or three tossed out whatever they had in their cups and, joining us at the table, opted for what I was pouring. They brought with them some cheese and more crackers, some grapes and vanilla cookies. In a few minutes we had a happy group of pilgrims sharing stories of their walk in several different languages and laughing together about anything and everything. The Architect would have been pleased.

The rosy-cheeked man and his wife were from Cologne and they told us that they sang in an *a cappella* chorale that had its beginnings in the middle ages. Everyone in the circle around the table begged them to sing something.

"Ya, ya, sing, sing! Sing for us!" one Swedish man pleaded. The Cologne Chorale duo looked at each other and quietly agreed on a song. Everyone sat very still. Even the passing traffic seemed

to stop. I had to catch my breath when their exquisite, clear voices rang out. The song they chose to sing—in German of course—was, "Amazing Grace."

Amazing Grace, how sweet the sound,
That saved a wretch like me.
I once was lost but now am found,
Was blind, but now, I see.

T'was Grace that taught,
my heart to fear.
And Grace, my fears relieved.
How precious did that Grace appear,
the hour I first believed.

Through many dangers, toils and snares,
we have already come.
T'was Grace that brought us safe thus far,
and Grace will lead us home.

The Lord has promised good to me.
His word my hope secures.
He will my shield and portion be,
as long as life endures.

When we've been here ten thousand years,
bright shining as the sun,
We've no less days to sing God's praise,
then when we've first begun.

Amazing Grace, how sweet the sound,
That saved a wretch like me.
I once was lost but now am found,
Was blind, but now, I see.

The irony of it completely overwhelmed me. I hadn't said anything about carrying Grace's ashes with me. I certainly hadn't mentioned my mother's name. They couldn't have known "Amazing Grace" was an epithet I had often used in referring to her.

When they had finished singing they looked at each other, clasped hands, and both breathed a deep sigh. No one moved or said a word. We sat with tears in our eyes, awe struck by the beauty of their singing. We all raised our glasses to them. Somewhere in the "coincidence" of their choice of a song, I sensed a good omen for the next phase of my walk.

And since you know you cannot see yourself,
so well as by reflection, I, your glass,
will modestly discover to yourself,
that of yourself which you yet know not of.

William Shakespeare

Astorga, with its partially encircling, undulating walls, spread out in the distance. I stood on a rise at Crucero de Santo Toribio, where I could see the cluster of buildings shining a pinkish white in the heat of the late afternoon. The towers and spires of the Bishop's Palace, an early design of Antonio Gaudí's, and the cathedral adjacent to it, offered a single ascending stone image.

Stopping again a couple of miles before arriving in Astorga in the small town of San Justo de la Vega, I bought something to eat at a roadside market. Standing in the shade of a tree near the store, I made a sandwich of canned *sardinellas* (sardines) and a soft, fragrant cheese with a crusty roll and ate it as I walked and took swigs from a large plastic bottle of deliciously cold sparkling water. I had already covered more than fifteen miles that day but I wanted to keep moving. There was always the daily worry of arriving at the *refugio* too late to find a bed available.

In San Martín that morning I had hurriedly made my way out of the *refugio* to avoid The Gruppo Spañiardos who had taken over the kitchen again. They were frying bread, making coffee and talking loud. It would have been impossible to sleep anyhow, so I set off in the early morning light hoping for the possibility of a cup of morning coffee of my own.

Hospital de Órbigo, almost five miles beyond San Martín, was the first town, village, or hamlet I reached where there was a bar. Actually, there were two or three. The signs on the doors all listed 9:30 as the opening hour. I dug for the watch I carried in my pants pocket— it read 8:45. I decided to station myself outside the door of the nicest looking bar, so I took off my backpack, lowered myself to the sidewalk and leaned up against the building—content to wait out the time doing some sketches and resting.

I was studying the treasured brochure I had picked up in León that listed the distances to the towns I was to pass through that day when the sound of a group of noisy people coming down the quiet, narrow street gave me a sense of panic. Yes, it was The Gruppo Spañiardos! They were heading for the very same bar where I was sitting! In a flash, I got up, donned my hat, put my pack on again, clipped the belt around my waist and made off to retrace my steps to where I had entered Hospital. In my haste to find coffee I had walked quickly over the spectacular ancient stone bridge that is Hospital de Órbigo's claim to fame. Since I had some time to kill, I decided to look more closely at what is said to be the oldest bridge in Spain. I would have thought the Roman bridges were far more ancient but maybe the distinction is that the bridge in Hospital de Órbigo is still intact and has been used continuously.

The *Puente de Paso Honroso* (Bridge of the Honorable Step) or *Puente de Piedra* (Bridge of Stone) spans more than 650 feet with twenty low, beautiful arches crossing the *Rio Órbigo*. The bridge continues beyond the limits of the river itself to a dry, flat stretch of land—probably a flood plain in the spring when the snow in the mountains melts and overwhelms this and other rivers in the region.

The name *Puente de Paso Honroso* refers to an event that happened in the middle ages when a knight, *Don Suero de Quiñones* challenged 300 other lance-baring knights to a joust to win the love of *Doña Leonora*, the daughter of Juan II and Isabella of Portugal. The town holds an annual re-enactment of the event in June where both townspeople and visitors dress in medieval costumes and parade across the bridge and through the small village on horseback. Some men actually do the jousting on the bridge as legend says the knight *Don Quiñones* did to win his love.

There was another cafe near the bridge that looked equally as pleasant as the first one I chose. As I opened the door, I could see that I would be the only customer. A small, dark-skinned young woman looked timidly at me. "*Buenos dias, señora.*" she said as she nodded her head in my direction. I ordered a *café con leché* and pointed to a picture over the counter where I sat that showed a plate of scrambled eggs wrapped in a kind of *tortilla*-like role with cheese melted on it. My diet was getting very boring. If you're a vegetarian, or at least don't eat meat, the Spanish cuisine leaves limited choices.

The television mounted over the counter showed tragedies and catastrophes going on all over the world. I looked away to shut out the images this time and ate my breakfast with pleasure. The taste of foods had become more distinct to me over the weeks of eating simple fare. When I did have a meal cooked and presented on a plate, I savored each mouthful in a way I can't say I had ever done before. For some reason—was it the cheese? special eggs?—the breakfast cooked and served to me that morning by the bashful woman of Hospital de Órbigo was one of the most memorable breakfasts of any I had on the Camino.

I stood to once again strap on my backpack and return to the day's walk. Digging into my money pouch, I took a few euros and paid the young woman. As I turned to smile and wave good-bye, she smiled and softly called out to me, "*Buen Camino, señora!*" as she bent to wipe the counter where I'd been sitting.

There's an option outside of Hospital de Órbigo to follow the highway again or take a more scenic path. I had learned my lesson with the day of highway walking out of León, so my choice was obvious. The weather was pleasantly warm but not yet as hot as it would be in a few hours. I enjoyed walking through the countryside dotted with small farms and fields of poppies, black-eyed susans, and a vast variety of flowers I didn't recognize and couldn't name. No other pilgrims were in sight for much of the walk. Occasionally I would look ahead to see one or two people walking with backpacks on but then, looking again later on, they weren't there. Possibly they had walked off the path to rest. I also saw some of the last stork's nests I would see along the Camino. The enormous birds weren't in sight but I could hear their chicks calling out as I passed near the huge nests built on the tops of utility poles.

A herd of sheep were walking straight toward me along a shady stretch of the path. There were at least a hundred of the soft, scruffy-looking, unshorn creatures. Their bleating, baa-baa chorus was loud and cacophonous. The throng crammed every visible foot of pathway and overflowed the boundaries on both sides. Large trees bordered and shaded the path—there was no getting around or through the sheep. They were standing extremely close to one another, and it seemed that all of their hooves couldn't possibly have touched the ground except maybe in a few strategic places where a select number of sheep were holding the group aloft. When they saw me, they stopped dead in their tracks. So did I. Their chatter stopped as well.

They looked like they could be spooked by just the slightest movement on my part. I was as much of a surprise to them as they were to me. I didn't have the slightest idea of how I would get beyond this impasse and thought I'd just stand very still for the moment. Their energy was very erratic. Thankfully, a young shepherd with a floppy hat and a big walking stick stepped out from behind them, tipped his hat to me and said *"Buenos días, señora!"* as he took the lead in front of the quivering mass. With a very slow and deliberate step, he led the sheep off the track and into an adjacent field. They scurried quickly behind him returning to their baa-baa chorus and, as they veered off in front of me, some glanced at me and seemed to look relieved to have been given a course to take. The sheep seemed a metaphor for humanity itself— fearful of the unknown, just looking for some direction.

The large building that was the *refugio* in Astorga had been a high school in its former life. The rooms were spacious and, where they had once been filled with desks and chalkboards, they were now filled with bunkbeds—no chalk to be seen. There were a couple of choices for a place to take a shower. I was warned by the manager when I signed in that most of the hot water was gone but that I could try the showers on the floor below the one where I should look for an available bed.

Thankfully, everyone was required to leave their boots outside the rooms on the stairwell landings, so the air in the rooms was breathable, aided by an entire wall of open windows. I took a lower bunk at the back of the room and across from an Australian man who made me laugh with everything he said. It was refreshing to be laughing so much even though his stories of how he got there weren't very funny.

He was traveling with his wife but she was no longer with him, having "stubbed her toe" and fallen down a mountain. (A bit of an exaggeration I learned.) She was in a hospital somewhere outside of Pamplona and besides, she had decided to leave him. "Enough was enough," she had told him. She couldn't remember why in the world she had agreed to walk all over Spain with him. She was going back to Melbourne as soon as she could walk again.

I laughed out loud when he hefted the black box that held Grace and exploded with, "Well, quite a hefty lady in her 'cinders.' Must have been a strapping broad in her 'bod!'" His irreverence was a relief from all the admiring looks with bowed heads and blessings I had been getting from anyone who heard what I was carrying with me in my backpack.

After I had settled my backpack under the bed I chose, I took the promised cold shower, dressed and napped then walked out to find a place in a nearby park to sit and draw in my journal.

The ancient wall around Astorga near the *refugio* enclosed the park with benches that looked out on the panorama of the countryside and the mountains in the distance. After a few minutes I became aware that I was seated with a group of elder townspeople who appeared as though they might meet on those benches regularly to spend the early evening hours talking together. Several men stood in a circle, some leaning on their canes, others talking passionately about—what? Politics, probably. An elegant lady with white hair, perfectly coiffed, sat next to me and tugged at the sweater she wore around her shoulders while at the same time, she waved a pretty black lace fan to stir up a breeze. She seemed genuinely disappointed when I smiled in response to her greeting and told her I didn't speak Spanish.

From my perch on the end of the bench, I could see snow on top of one of the mountains to the west. I shuddered to think of the possibility that I might soon be climbing into that kind of cold. The idea was at once exhilarating coming from the heat of the past weeks and a bit worrying since I had no warm clothes. Resolved to deal with that as I came to it, I wandered off to look around the city.

Astorga has Roman origins and was strategic to their transporting the ore they mined in the mountains that bordered the western horizon. For centuries the city also served as a major stopping place for pilgrims to rest, buy supplies and regroup before starting the climb into those same mountains. The *Camino Francés* (the major Camino de Santiago) and another path used by pilgrims, the *Via de la Plata*, or "Silver Path," meet in Astorga. Originally an ancient trade route, the *Via de la Plata*, connects Seville in the south with Astorga where it joins the Camino and continues west to Santiago.

The Gaudí Episcopal Bishop's Palace was built in the late 19th century and looks like it could have served as a model for the Disney castle. The multi-spired building is now a museum dedicated to the

Camino de Santiago, the *Museo de los Caminos*. The collection also includes Roman archeological artifacts. Once again, however, I arrived too late to visit. The museum had closed earlier for the day and I didn't want to delay my walk the next day to be there when it re-opened. Just one more day to Rabanal del Camino and then, the following day, the *Cruz de Ferro*. *I'm going to make it!* I told myself, with an inward sense of relief. My strength was holding up in large part because I was being more careful about having enough water and food to keep me going.

Later that evening, The Two French Women Who Never Smile were the last to arrive in my chosen room at the *refugio*. One of the sullen young ladies took the bunk above The Australian Comic; the other took the one above me. They were always together on the trail when I passed them, or they passed me. They never smiled at anyone and spoke only to each other. When we were all later settled into our beds that night, they tried to fit in one bed (over the Australian, thankfully) but quickly realized that wasn't going to work when the Australian pointed out the tenuous nature of the beds.

"Hey there you above! You two are cauzin' quite a bulge down this way. I don't wanna' look like a waffle when those springs come down and plasta' me to the floor!"

Reluctantly, one of the ladies came back to the bed above me and they held hands across the gap between. During the night, when they had let go of each other, the woman above me tossed and turned so much that I was reminded of the first night at Roncesvalles when The Australian Chef was kept awake by The Irish Priest's tossings. After an hour or more of being rocked around, I grabbed my sleeping bag and the light mattress on the bed and dragged them to the floor in front of the windows where I finally fell asleep.

Slowly over the days and weeks that I had been walking, and thinking about Grace—her life, her instability, her emotional and physical abuses, and her unhappiness—I had found a sense of peace and understanding that I don't believe I could have come to without this ultimate walk with her. What I had always seen as Grace's short-comings, were in the end the very things that gave me my strengths. And, for all of those strengths, I'm very grateful.

Her influence on me was profound, even though we weren't close the way other mothers and daughters often are. Her influence was in the contrasts she offered me. Knowing what I did not want to be, to have, to become, helped me see what I did want. I challenged myself and at times, stumbling as I went, I chose my own way of life, sometimes because of what she did do but most often because of what she didn't do. In either case, her influence permeated every area of my life.

My decision to study art was in large part because of Grace. Her near reverence for her father and his artistic talents no doubt created a a desire for me to have that same sort of admiration from her. The admiration never came, but my interests and talents probably wouldn't have given me any other choice but to have a life that somehow involved me in the arts.

To her credit she would often point out the beauty in nature—the loveliness of a sunset, the tenderness of a flower. One would think that kind of sensitivity was out of keeping with her sometimes coarse and thoughtless way of dealing with others; but she loved to look at beautiful things and I think Nature calmed her. She was also usually making something, sewing something, or cooking up a new recipe. Her creativity was boundless and even in her last years, when she was almost completely blind, she continued to enjoy making beaded necklaces and Christmas ornaments—things that kept her fingers busy and her mind focused.

She sometimes mentioned a nameless woman she admired who had studied at Pratt Institute and who had taught her a few stylistic and practical dressmaking and fashion tips. She never suggested it as a place where I could study art but when I was about to finish high school, I sent for an entrance application and started working on a portfolio for acceptance. I had no training and wasn't even enrolled in an art class in high school. I also hadn't the slightest idea of how to go about taking the SAT test needed for acceptance. Most importantly, I hadn't had any discussion with my parents about their willingness to help me pay for tuition if I did get accepted. And, for some unfathomable reason, I was indeed accepted at Pratt that fall.

On my own at eighteen, I found a small, two-room apartment on the top floor of a brownstone in Brooklyn, around the corner from campus. With a wide-ranging, broad-based variety of jobs and some loans, I persisted through to my degree five years later. Those five years were formative and exciting. They were also frightening and at times very lonely. I'm glad now that I lived that complicated, demanding time. The creative environment at Pratt and the artists and others I met there made an immeasurable impact on the trajectory of my life.

While she would probably present herself as a pragmatist, Grace had a love of the dramatic and the romantic. She enjoyed watching dance and musical theater and she took me to see musicals on a couple of occasions. One day in the last years of her life, we were sitting in her small room at the nursing home where she was living, watching a musical on television together and she began to describe her life at home with her parents and aunts and grandparents. She recalled how often they would all take part in staging operettas or small plays to entertain one another. It was most often her aunts and grandmother who would design and sew the costumes. The aunts starred in the leading roles, sang operatic parts and danced as well. It was comforting to me to know that she could remember such happy childhood times.

During the last week of her life, Grace remained in her bed in her room in a nursing home outside of Washington, D.C. Sometimes I slept on the reclining chair a nurse had rolled into the room for me. I spoke with her even though she didn't answer—I was sure she heard me. One day, I remember saying, "Well, Mom, it looks like you're getting ready to leave me, huh?" and much to my surprise, with her eyes still closed, she replied, "I'll never leave you, Maureen." A sentiment I didn't appreciate at the time.

I brought her milk shakes every day to give her something to sustain herself with as she lay still, not otherwise eating; not opening her eyes; not saying anything. She recognized that I was there and hungrily sucked on the straw I touched to her lips. She hadn't eaten anything sweet for a long time—she had diabetes. I decided the sugar restriction didn't really matter anymore and asked the nurses to stop annoying her with taking blood samples.

On what was to be one of her last days, as I entered her room, her head turned in my direction in recognition that I was there. She haltingly said, "I want to stand . . ." There was a long pause during which I wondered how I was going to help her do that, and then she continued, "...and bow to you." There it was—the recognition I had so long sought from her was in her last, halting words to me.

She said "yes" when I asked if she would like to see my son, Michael. He arrived on the train from New York around noon. She was aware of his presence and opened her sightless eyes as if to say "hello" to him when he entered her room. We spent the day seated on either side of her bed, each of us holding one of her hands. It was as if Grace was a conduit that our conversation flowed through. She seemed comforted by our quiet talk of other things. At times, Michael spoke tenderly, directly to her. He kissed her cheek and told her good-bye when he stood to leave the room. She died a few hours after I drove him to Union Station to catch a late train back to New York. I wasn't there. I had decided to go home and sleep in my own bed that night.

Leaving the flat plains of the *meseta* was a relief after the monotony of the terrain. A young British pilgrim I had met the night before leaving Astorga told me that his handbook from the Confraternity of Saint James described the walk from Astorga to Ponferrada as the most beautiful and the most difficult. We had both sat down at neighboring tables in a cafe in the plaza in front of the cathedral to have a glass of wine. As I ordered a piece of the sweet bread, *mantecada*, which Astorga is known for, he explained that we will have climbed to almost 5,000 feet between where we sat (at 2,800 feet or 890 m) and our arrival in Ponferrada. Somehow, the math didn't add up for me but I didn't question him. I did know the highest point of the thirty-five mile stretch of mountains and passes between the two cities is on *Monte Irago*, at 4,977 feet or 1517 meters, in fact, the highest elevation on the entire Camino where there is a military base and the *Cruz de Ferro*.

Out beyond ideas of wrongdoing and rightdoing,
there is a field. I'll meet you there.

When the soul lies down in that grass,
the world is too full to talk about.
Ideas, language, even the phrase *each other*
doesn't make any sense.

Rumi

Armed with those impressive statistics about the path ahead, I walked out just before dawn the next morning to begin the ascent into the mountains that would take me through the region known as *La Maragatería*. Astorga is the unofficial capitol of this unique ethnic and geographical area that includes the mountains and an extended area to the south.

Leaving the more populated part of the province of Castillia-León with all of its political graffiti and separatist sentiments—*"ESPAGNA, NO! CASTILLIA-LEON, SI!"* and *"LIBRE CASTILLIA!"*—the path enters the beautiful mountainous countryside. Strewn with the ruins of many villages, settlements and hamlets, stone buildings with collapsed roofs, the broken wooden stalls of a farm yard, stables, even churches lie in piles of rubble at either side of the path. At times there was one lone inhabitable house in a whole village of rubble. On two occasions, I saw dogs barking fiercely; one was chained to a derelict hovel, another to a crumbling stable. The Spanish Resistance during the time of Franco was known to have hidden out in some of the abandoned settlements that lay along the Camino. Later that day at Rabanal another pilgrim speculated that the freedom fighters most likely used the then seldom-walked Camino path itself to reach the safety of their hideouts.

The people of *La Maragatería* are said to be quite unique in a variety of ways. They have dress, food and traditions unlike people in other regions of Spain. Although I never found anyone who could describe just what those unique characteristics were, I did learn that they actually have a specific gene that continues to convey to present day off-spring. The *Maragatos* were the early muleteers who deftly carried cargo over and through the mountainous trails before there were other forms of transportation.

I didn't meet anyone along the path who distinguished himself in looks or dress but I did begin to see a difference in the way the houses were built—both standing and not standing. There was a more common second story that had an overhanging porch made of wood. On some of the narrow roads through the empty villages it looked like people could actually have handed things across to each other from one side of the street to the other. Certainly those overhangs would have been important lookout positions to watch for anyone entering the roads and byways.

The well-known, semi-deserted town of El Ganso arrived early in the day. It has three bars, right next to each other all with signs in Spanish and English hoping to attract the passing pilgrims away from their neighbors. The "Bar Cowboy," had several colorful handwritten signs outside giving the menu of the day, the promise of a pilgrim stamp for your passport, and enough antennas on the roof to guarantee a television. Since it was late morning, I decided to have a lunch served on a plate rather than my usual handmade, hand-held, "snack" sort of meal.

The walls of the small room were lined with American cowboy movie posters of John Wayne, Gene Autry and Clint Eastwood. Two local men stood at the bar talking to the bartender who, judging from the pride he took in welcoming me, must have been the owner of the place. I got an especially warm response when I told the men I was American.

As I waited for my lunch to arrive, one of the sun-darkened, middle aged men walked over to my table and told me in broken English that he had not seen many Americans on the trail before the last few years.

"I never see American women who make walk alone," he said, shaking his head back and forth. "You not afraid?"

"Well, I just don't think about being afraid. So, I'm not."

"Humph," he said, raising his chin in the air and looking at me with squinting eyes.

He had lived in El Ganso all his life and, as he spoke more, even with his bad teeth and his bent body, I began to realize that he wasn't middle aged at all but more likely only in his mid-thirties.

My standard egg and potato *tortilla* came with a salad of wilted greens, a blob of spicy salsa and a single chili pepper. An ice-cold beer I drank from the bottle washed it down. Something that looked like a soap opera was on the television hanging on the wall over the bar. Two other pilgrims entered Bar Cowboy, nodded to me, and smiled at the posters as they took off their backpacks and settled into chairs at a table on the other side of the room. It was already too late in the day to sit at one of the small plastic tables baking outside in the sun.

The dry, dusty paths and roadways leading into and out of El Ganso were typical of the roads all along the walk that day. Looking off to a field rising to my right as I left the Cowboys, I saw a woman in a dark patterned dress walking in the rows of recently turned dry earth. Her back was toward me but I could see she wore an apron tied around her waist and she held a black umbrella in one of her hands as she extended the other one almost as though she were walking a tight rope. Stepping slowly, she placed each foot gracefully on the dusty earth beneath her. The heat of the midday sun was intense. A dog scampered around her, barking and wagging its tail. Her thick-set body belied the youthful elegance in her stride.

The distance to Rabanal del Camino from Astorga was less than eleven and a half miles but I decided to stop for the night in Rabanal even though I didn't think I had walked very far that day. The ascent from Rabanal to the *Cruz de Ferro* would be something to look forward to the next morning,

It was a long slow climb to Rabanal, much of which was alongside a two lane, paved road. Thankfully, there weren't many cars. A young couple rode slowly by me on their bicycles and, from their greeting, I could tell they were Americans, and, from their accents, most likely New Yorkers. Both were short and heavy, and both were sporting incredibly painful looking sunburns. After they realized I too was American, they stopped and got off their bikes to walk along with me through a particularly steep section of the road.

This was their second pilgrimage on the Camino; they didn't look fit enough to be such devotees. The first time they covered the route, two years before, they had also traveled by bicycle. On that trip, they had stayed at a small hostel in Rabanal (shunning all *refugios* for the lack of privacy).

"Oh, you should definitely go there. It's a nice place. Clean. Very clean! They have almost-American bathrooms and good food in the restaurant. Good price, too."

They had called ahead a few days before and made reservations to stay there themselves. I waved and thanked them for the tip as they mounted their bikes and rode off. "See you there! *Buen Camino!*" they both shouted back.

I had been looking forward to staying at one of the *refugios* in Rabanal del Camino. One of the three that I had heard were in the tiny hamlet, the *Refugio Gaucelmo*, was housed in a 12th century building—recently restored by the British organization, The Confraternity of St. James. The group's work to spread knowledge of the Camino is internationally known and I wanted to support their efforts. I thought, too, it would be a comfort to have so many English speakers to talk with.

When I finally reached Rabanal and walked around the few dusty roads that make up the center, I easily found the *Refugio Gaucelmo*. It was distinguished by a string of pilgrims already queued-up and waiting to enter when the doors opened in about an hour's time. Among those waiting were The Two French Women Who Never Smile, looking gloomy as they both turned and seemed to glare at me. I shook off the sense of dread I had when I thought of the possibility of having to share a bunk with one or the other of them again as I had in Astorga. Another sleepless night was out of the question! The fear propelled me in pursuit of the hostel recommended by The Bicyclists from New York.

The room I was given at the top of the three-story building gave me a sense of privacy that I hadn't felt since staying at the *hospitaleria* in Santo Domingo. I relished the long, hot shower and a chance to thoroughly shampoo my hair. I dried myself with the fresh towels and left my dirty clothes to soak in the bathtub while I laid down for my *siesta*. Feeling clean and pleasantly languorous, I spread out fully on the wide, comfortable bed that fit into the small room with only enough additional space to stand and walk around it. A skylight window was directly over my head and as I was dozing off, I thought that later that night I just might get to see the Milky Way after all.

CARRYING GRACE TO SANTIAGO

I woke with a start. *What time is it?* There was just enough time to get to the Pilgrim's Service that was held in the small Santa Maria chapel, across from the *refugio*. I dressed quickly, twisted my damp hair into a ponytail, dashed down the two flights of stairs and out onto the dusty street.

Several of the pilgrims in Astorga said that the service at Rabanal was not to be missed. The few Benedictine brothers who live in the monastery of *San Salvador de Monte Irago*, next to the *refugio*, conduct the service. Along with blessing pilgrims, they would bless stones to be left at the *Cruz de Ferro* and, unique to any of the services I had seen, they sang chants. I was anxious to hear the music and originally I thought I would carry Grace with me to the service but, at the last minute, I decided not to bring the black box.

A group of ten or twelve pilgrims were already seated when I entered the quiet candle lit room. The patched and pealing walls caught the golden glow of the candles. In a small area at the front of the Romanesque building there was a simple altar that held a vase of wild flowers. Chairs were placed on either side of the altar where I anticipated the monks would sit.

As we waited for the service to begin, I noticed the couple that had sung "Amazing Grace" in San Martín. They were seated across the aisle from me. I smiled in their direction and they nodded. Looking away, I was once again surprised by the sound of their exquisite voices rising out of the hush of the chapel, and swung my head back to see them, still seated as they began their song. The hymn they chose was familiar although I couldn't name it. Everyone was obviously moved by the dulcet tones of their voices—singing *a cappella*, so appropriately. We all sat very still—many wiped away tears. When they stopped singing, I think I wasn't alone in wanting to stand and applaud them but, the monks had arrived and the Pilgrim's Service began.

The several languages that the service was presented in were punctuated by the melodic chants of the three young men who stood at either side of the altar. The curve of the apse behind them played a part in the illusion that there were many more voices than just their three. One of the men who looked a bit older than the others, lead the service. His words in English sent a chill through me when he spoke of "carrying Grace to the top of the mountain where we will be closer to God." *How could he know?*

Before going back to my room, I walked around Rabanal's few streets and stopped to talk with The Cologne Chorale as they strolled toward me.

"Hello, dear people!" I greeted. "Thank you so much for your beautiful song! I was so moved—again. After the service, people were saying your singing is like angels from heaven!"

We decided to go somewhere to have a drink together and walked to the end of the town where there was a bar and restaurant. We were the only people in the room so we seated ourselves and expected someone would show up soon and take our order. I learned that their names were Paul and Delphini and we talked, as all pilgrims do, about our experiences since we had last seen one another. We spent an hour or so over drinks that were served by a young man who explained they didn't have any snacks as Paul had hoped. They wouldn't let me pay the tab, so I left them still feeling a sense of gratitude that had no outlet.

Since the sun doesn't set in northern Spain until well after the hour that I wanted to go to bed, I tried to wake myself in the middle of the night to peer out of the skylight above my bed and look for the Milky Way. Granted, I was groggy when I woke, but I cannot claim to be a witness to the Camino and its relationship to the Milky Way.

In preparation for the day ahead—the final climb to the *Cruz de Ferro*—the next morning I decided to have a good breakfast at the small cafe in the hostel. The added anticipated emotional stress of whatever my final goodbye to Grace would be, left me a little anxious. I wanted to feel prepared.

The Bicyclists from New York were just finishing their breakfast as I sat down at a small wooden table opposite them in the dining area of the cafe.

"So, you decided to stay here! How'd you like it? Nice, huh?" the young woman greeted me with a smile of satisfaction. "We didn't steer ya' wrong, did we? Huh?"

"No, you didn't! I enjoyed the rest very much. And the shower, Oh! It was great to sleep on a nice wide bed, too!" I effused.

"Good. Good. I'm glad."

Well, we're off," she said as they both stood up from their table and she donned her cycling hat. "Gotta' get movin' before it gets too hot!" She waved to me again as her husband paid the check. He had kept his head down throughout our exchange and seemed irritated about something. He raised it briefly and nodded in my direction as he muttered, "*Buen Camino*," then pushed the outside door open, letting the bright light and warm air momentarily flood the cool dark room.

After breakfast, and settling my bill, I rested my backpack on the chair next to me and hoisted it up once again to make the final climb to the *Cruz de Ferro*. I walked out into the bright sunshine and followed the road to the end where the Camino markers were obvious. The bells from the chapel where the pilgrim's service was held the night before were chiming eight o'clock. Just at the edge of the town itself, I saw an elderly man standing in front of his small stucco house, tending to some weeds with one hand as he leaned down on a cane with the other. He was wearing a bright red sweater that was buttoned over a patterned shirt. He stood up as I passed him, took off his black beret hat, and with a courtly gesture, he smiled and bowed as he said, "*Buenos dias, señora!*" Somehow, I felt it would be.

The very first "guide" to the Camino was written by Aymery Picard, a French monk who stayed at the *Refugio Gaucelmo*. That was not the one in Rabanal, however, run by the Confraternity of St. James but the original one that had been built by a 12th century religious hermit, Gaucelmo, who received permission from the king to build the hospice and a church for the pilgrims at Foncebadón. The now abandoned town is about three and a half miles up the mountain from Rabanal. Today, what's left of the hospice and the church is little more than a pile of stones, arranged along a simple dirt path that describes the town of Foncebadón. The electric lines that hang limply from pole to pole and one or two streetlights are the only evidence that there is life remaining among the ruins. Indeed, there are now two small restaurants and a *refugio* that serves food which is said to be quite good.

I had planned to have a second cup of coffee at one of the dilapidated Foncebadón eateries but, as the clouds started to cover the hillside and the roadway where I walked, I reconsidered and determined, instead, to keep going before any bad weather rolled in. The overcast skies gave me a melancholy feeling and the look of impending rain hurried me along a little more. At breakfast in Rabanal I was told I would reach the *Cruz de Ferro* in an hour but it was taking me nearly two and a half hours to climb the five miles. I couldn't come up with an explanation as to why time was dragging so much.

Finally I arrived at a place where the Camino path veered from the road and brought me in sight of the *Cruz de Ferro*. There it was. Right there in front of me. *Could this be possible? I made it!*

The massive mound of rocks and shells encircled a towering timber that held the rusting iron cross. It was still off in the distance a bit but, when I saw it, I stood completely still. I wanted to take it all in. The gray scene gave me an eerie sense of gloom. I was disappointed to see that the main road went directly by the cross and that there were parking lots around for cars and buses to pull off. I imagined that later in the day hoards of people would be driven to this remote mountain top and they would be disgorged to roam about the site, picnic, and have their pictures taken as proof that they had seen this ancient sacred place.

Many people were already sitting around on the ground, trying to stay out of the wind. Some were eating and resting on the available picnic benches. Wisps of clouds floated around the clearing. Bike riders who had made it up the mountain on their bikes were now running up the mound of crushed stones and shells to have their photos taken while standing next to the mammoth beam. Graffiti covered the outside of the one-room, stone chapel that stood to the rear of the mound. I sat to rest on the grass near the chapel, hoping the picnickers would leave. The chapel was closed with an iron gate that was locked but allowed a view to the inside. There was little to see though—a cross, a table, some dead flowers, notes (prayers perhaps?) written on bits of paper and thrown inside now littering the floor.

A young, dark haired woman I had seen leaning on a walking stick, standing outside of the Confraternity *refugio* in Rabanal had already arrived. *How could she have gotten here before me?* I wondered. She was sitting on a bench that was built up against the outside wall of the chapel and under the overhang of the sloping roof. I had noticed her on the trail several days before as well. She had an angelic face and was quite over weight with short dark hair, artlessly cut into a mannish style. She walked alone with the aid of elastic supports on both of her knees and a large wooden cross that hung around her neck. I had the impression that she might be a nun. She had the habit of frequently pushing her thick glasses up on her nose. The gesture made her look studious and maybe more serious than her youth suggested.

She watched me as I went to the pile with the stones and shells that friends had given me to place on that ancient pile for them. I

repeated each friend's name as I placed their easily identifiable talismans into the mass. Then I turned to go back to where I had rested my backpack on the ground against a tree. I lifted out the black box that held Grace's ashes. Once again, I walked to the pile, this time choosing a quiet side, near a bush that was growing from somewhere within the edge of the stones. I didn't want anyone to walk over Grace on their way to have a picture taken.

I knelt down in front of the mound and, for the first time, I took the lid off the box. Inside was a plastic bag full of white powdered dust that was closed with a twister tie. It all seemed so bizarre to me that this heavy plastic bag with its contents of cinders was all that represented Grace. I was uncomfortable putting my hand into the bag so I lifted it out of the box, undid the tie and poured some of the ashes near the bush. The breeze was taking wisps of the ash out of the bag and I tried to contain the escaping powder with my hands. There were bits of bone, left somewhat as shards. In the end, my hands were covered with her ashes as I finally let the last bit go.

My body was trembling as I stood holding onto the empty plastic bag. I kept rubbing my hands together and trying to wipe off the dusty, clinging remains. I felt oddly removed from myself and my actions, as if I were watching the scene from somewhere else. I bowed my head and said out loud, "Good-bye, Grace. I hope you've found peace. Thank you for all you tried to do for me. Thank you for teaching me to be patient and thank you for giving me the desire to understand." Tears gathering in my eyes obscured the gray and colorless scene. Images of Grace rushed through my mind: her face when it was young and beautiful; her, standing over me as a child with hands on her hips; her, in scenes of Christmases past; her, in old age bent over her beading. *Good-bye, Grace*, I repeated to myself.

It was done. I had accomplished what I had come to do. I stood up and turned slowly, as if in a trance. I carried the empty black box and plastic bag back to where I had left my backpack. The heavy-set young woman still sat on the bench alongside the chapel. Knowingly, she smiled softly at me as I walked closer to her, then she crossed herself and nodded. I nodded back as I wiped the tears from my eyes with my sleeve.

Was that it? Was that all there was going to be to it? I wished The Cologne Chorale singers had been there to sing for Grace or even The Singing Señoritas from the early days of my walk who woke every morning with a song. I wished The Dutch Couple Who Picnic had gathered around me with their calm and encouraging natures. A silent embrace from Diana from Quebec would have soothed me. I was certain The Irish Priest would have said something meaningful and appropriate. It would have been wonderful to have The Architect, The Mexican Boy Scouts and Hanna and Horst to share my ceremony with—to make it somehow more memorable, more important. The young nun, however, would be my only witness.

It was difficult for me to get my things together. My hands were still trembling, I sat cross-legged on the ground rearranging the contents of my backpack, then rose to walk slowly to a refuse bin where I dropped the black box that had been such a constant and heavy presence. Returning to where I had left it, I bent down to hoist my much lighter backpack up and, putting an arm through a strap, I grabbed the other one easily and buckled the belt tight around my waist. I stood wobbling in place for a moment, looking off toward the bush where I had left Grace. It was time for me to move on. I had laid down my burden and now longed to feel the wings The Irish Priest assured me of. It was clear the wings were not yet available to me, however. With shaky legs, I crossed the road to look for the markers that would lead me forward on my journey, back to the Camino and the descent from that cloud-shrouded mountain top.

When you eventually see through the
veils to how things really are,
you will keep saying again and again,
"This is certainly not the way we
thought it was!"

Rumi

The descent from the top of the mountain was treacherous. There were no sizable trees, only scrub bushes and clumps of brambles. The path was strewn with loose shale and gravel, making every step precarious. A cool wind blew sharp gusts of dirt in my eyes. The overcast skies and low-lying clouds gave only momentary views of the landscape to the west. It was hard to judge how far down the decent went before it evened off.

That morning, a head cold that came on in León had blossomed into a runny nose and an annoying, constant cough. The events of the morning had taken a lot of my strength and, as usual, I was very hungry. El Acebo, a village a little less than six miles ahead, was going to be my destination for the day—if I could only make it that far. I longed to just sit down and slide there.

Anyone with aching knees will agree that going downhill is much more difficult than climbing up. The constant shock to my knee joints made the long descent seemingly endless. At least a dozen times I stood aside on the narrow path to allow groups of walkers to get around me. They scudded by, hardly seeming to touch the ground—obviously elated to have passed the famous landmark—and well on their way to Santiago. *"Buen Camino," "Buen Camino," "Buen Camino,"* they all sang out as they passed. When were those wings The Irish Priest promised me going to sprout? My backpack was undeniably lighter, but I was still not experiencing the sense of relief I had been counting on after leaving Grace on that summit.

Smoke was rising from a small chimney as I neared the outpost of Tomás, "the last Knight Templar." His hut and rickety outbuildings with colorful signs, all hammered up in various directions, were at a turn on the path called, Manjarin. The place is yet another site of an abandoned village. Here Tomás has created a shelter where he dedicates himself to caring for pilgrims. He provides meals, sometimes cooked at his outdoor kitchen, and in the evenings he sings Gregorian chants. I was told he gives healings and massages to any weary traveler who asks. Knight Tomás maintains about twenty beds and has no set fees for the shelter or the food but does accept donations.

My brother and I used to like to create "forts" and hiding places with the cushions from the sofa and my father's favorite wing chair. Sometimes with a blanket thrown over the top, we made tunnels and roadways that we could crawl through to reach each other's stronghold. Many rainy afternoons we spent in battles defending our territory and trying to take the other's position. My dolls served as lookouts and defenders of my "castle" and Frank's planes and battleships were there to swoop in and destroy my post—complete with sound effects.

I had wanted to stop to meet Tomás, a true legend of the path, to compare his fort with those of my childhood, or just to look into the cave-like hut, draped with a ragged blanket. Smoke was also slowly drifting up from a campfire somewhere just beyond where a group of people stood talking, leaning on their walking sticks, looking very much like sentries. Maybe Tomás was having as much fun as my brother and I had. I didn't stop, though. My mood didn't allow for anyone else's fantasies. It all seemed a bit staged to me. Judging from my quick glance into Tomás' domain, I felt it didn't compare with what Frank and I plucked from our imaginations on those rainy afternoons.

Somewhere I read there's a point on the trail that's actually higher than the place where the *Cruz de Ferro* is but I have no memory of it. I can only remember going down, down, down and into semi-deserted El Acebo. That was my limit for the day. I wanted to find a place to eat a hot and, hopefully, delicious meal. Maybe I'd even order some wine and toast the success of my mission.

As I entered a bar to the left of the path, which cuts straight through the desolate town, I was immediately asked by the woman near the entrance if I wanted a bed for the night and, if I did, I should go upstairs and claim it (there were only three remaining, she explained) and then return to eat. When I reappeared without my backpack, the woman at the door waved me into a modest dining room at the back of the small building. I chose a table in the middle of the room. She handed me a menu and then disappeared. Patiently, and with long, deep breaths, I tried to decipher the names of the Spanish foods with the help of the pocket dictionary I had fished out of my backpack before coming down for lunch.

"May I help you with the menu?" said a dark and handsome man who was sitting at the table behind me. Did my constant sighs of frustration give me away? His woman companion had just left the table and was returning with extra napkins.

"Oh, would you? That would be great!" I laughed with relief. He spoke in heavily accented English. I thought he was either Italian or Spanish. His friend, who turned out to be his wife, was American and stood a good head taller than he.

The two were in their forties and both were tan and in great condition, well-rested, and wearing stylish shorts and shirts—not wrinkled and faded as many pilgrim's clothes were at this point on the trail. They came over to my table and, standing behind and on either side of me, began to translate the menu. In a chorus, with corrections to each other and ever more precise details, they gave me an almost complete rundown of the entire menu. More than I bargained for. It was clearly a competition.

"Yes, there is some fish but, no, no, you don't want this fish," he said.

"Maybe they can make you an omelette?" she said. "Oh! Yes, understood; too many omelettes is not good. Boring, besides."

"You sure you couldn't eat just a little chicken, just this one time?" he cajoled.

I settled on hot vegetable soup, the fish (which turned out to be delicious), and a crunchy, fresh green salad—a rare treat.

The "Menu Diviners" invited me to join them at their table. As I stood and walked back to their table with them, I told them I was celebrating, and filled them in on my successful mission. The man poured me a glass of wine from their bottle and we all raised our glasses. "To Grace!" we said in unison.

Gianluca, was a native of Madrid and a former soccer player and she, Susan, was an American businesswoman working for a corporation in Lucerne, Switzerland. They had met in a bar in Madrid and were married less than a year later. They considered "home" their house on the southern coast of Spain—away from the cold of winter—where they spent as much time as they could with his much beloved dogs—at least two, if I remember correctly. In the summers, they went to the States. This was her third and his sixth walk on the Camino. They liked to walk it every spring, "To get our heads screwed on right," Susan said.

Susan recommended a *refugio* in Triacastela a few days walk ahead, in the province of Galicia. They usually preferred the privacy of hostels, hotels and even an occasional *parador* but they liked the Triacastela *refugio*. It was owned by an architect from Bilbao, the town where the new Guggenheim museum is, and it was managed by a woman who spoke some English. They have a coin-operated washing machine there and clean bathrooms with plenty of hot water. "It's a popular place," she warned, "so get there early."

Gianluca took a pause in his ravenous attack on the plate of delicious smelling sausage the waitress had set in front of him.

"You're staying here tonight?" he asked. "Hmm, I understand," he said when I explained I was too tired to go any further. "We're going on to Molinaseca after lunch. Some friends are meeting us there for dinner later."

We chatted aimlessly through lunch, touching on mutually interesting topics like travel in general, the political climate of Spain, and the war in Iraq. None of us really wanted to be reminded of the war so the conversation moved quickly to the care and keeping of the Camino and the people we'd met along the way—always an agreeable topic.

After our leisurely lunch, we walked together to the door and I stepped outside with them into the hot sun. I stood shading my eyes with my hand and watched as they donned their backpacks and helped each other with adjustments. Susan put on her Red Sox baseball cap and Gianluca tied a bandanna around his neck.

"Thanks for being part of my celebration!" I said as I waved "*Buen Camino*" with my free hand. They turned and walked on, waving as they went. As it was with so many people I met, spent time with, and enjoyed so fully, I knew I would probably never see them again. I went back inside, crossed the room where the bar was and slowly mounted the stairs to my waiting bed.

After lunch that afternoon, I took a five-hour nap, then a shower, and then back to my bunk to sleep for another nine hours. Most of my sleep though was interrupted with coughing and sneezing into wads of tissue I'd burgled from the toilet. The bunkbeds at that *refugio* had been pushed up against each other so that the person in the next bed felt like a sleeping partner. I thought I'd spare the woman next to me the nuisance of my sneezing and hung my towel/wrap-up cloth between us, tucking it beneath the mattress above me. Actually, it gave me the first sense of privacy I'd felt in one of those bunks and I wondered why I hadn't thought of it before.

The next morning coffee was available in the restaurant downstairs so I started the day with coffee and a fried sweet roll. As I was passing the last of the crumbling houses of El Ascebo I saw an elderly man ahead of me. He was shooing some sheep from the path with his walking stick. Just as in the morning greeting I had in Rabanal, when I was a few steps from the elderly gentleman, he took off his crumpled hat and said cheerfully, *"Buenos dias, señora!"* Again, I had every reason to believe it would be: My pack was lighter, my "mission" had been accomplished and I was fed and well rested. The remaining miles of the walk would be just walking to Santiago, with no other agenda. Grace had her final resting place and I was just happy to be moving along— wings or no wings.

Somewhere on the stretch from El Acebo to Ponferrada there's said to be a hermit living near the path who gives foot massages to pilgrims. I kept glancing off to the right and left as I went along to see if I could spot where the hermit was living. My toes were heavily bandaged in the places where I had lost toenails but I had no new blisters and the thought of getting a relaxing foot massage was spurring me on. The only place I saw that might have been the hermit's home, however, was a spot under a large tree where an old, dirty, clear plastic tent was set up. A car seat was out in front of the tent. No one appeared to be home. A lot of pieces of paper were tucked into a rope that was wrapped around the tree and the scraps of paper had messages written in at least four languages that I could make out. No hermit; alas, no foot massage.

The descent into Molinaseca was another steep and precarious one. It was just over five miles from El Acebo and it took me almost three hours to walk there. The small village was a beautiful respite from the disintegrating villages I'd seen over the last few days. I understood why Susan and Gianluca wanted to walk on from El Acebo and spend the night there. It had a small river, (a tributary to the *Rio Sil* that cuts through Ponferrada) a Roman bridge, flowers everywhere, charming houses with gardens and a lovely old church. I stopped to talk with another pilgrim in the town center and he said he'd heard Molinaseca had become a weekend retreat for families and business people from Ponferrada only a few miles away by car. The influx of tourists and second-home owners as well as the fact that it's on a paved road saved Molinaseca from being another deserted mountain village.

Ponferrada by contrast is a bustling city of nearly 60,000, with its own nuclear reactor plant that could be seen from the mountains above Molinaseca. Its name ("iron bridge") derives from the 11th century bridge that was built for the pilgrims to cross the *Rio Sil* that meanders south through the valley. The highlight of the old section of Ponferrada is the ruins of the castle of the Knights Templar, which has undergone a lot of restoration in recent years. It rises majestically as you enter the medieval quarter.

The signage for the Camino (and for the *refugio*) wasn't great, so I spent time wandering around the old section looking for a clue. The Cologne Chorale, were just exiting the cathedral as I passed. They were on their way out of Ponferrada and stopped to chat as they headed off. Before leaving, they pointed me in the direction for THE *refugio*.

"Oh, now, you must stay at that new *refugio* on the edge of town," Paul exclaimed. "It is the best on the whole Camino. Wonderful rooms, new beds—very comfortable. You're going to love it!"

A Swiss businessman who had walked to Santiago himself had built the "new" *refugio* a few years before. He felt his life had been so transformed by the experience that he bought the land and had the *refugio* built in appreciation for what the walk had meant to him.

The *Albergue San Nicolas de Flüe* is situated on the edge of what looked like a soon-to-be new development of buildings. It was for the time though, across from a vacant field and near no other buildings, shops, or houses. Even as I entered the iron gate, I wasn't sure I'd arrived at the right place until I looked to my right and saw the name of the place sculpted out of ironwork which was set in the wall, "*Albergue de Pelegrinos - S. Nicolas de Flüe*," Hotel of Pilgrims - St. Nicolas de Flüe.

Except for an old chapel-like building at the left of the entrance, the *refugio* itself was new and open in design. It was built in a U-shape with a small pool and bubbling fountain at the center of the "U." The pool was rectangular and had a broad stone edge that provided seating to anyone wanting to sit and soak their feet in the cool water. As I walked past it and into the main door to register, several people were doing just that— sitting with their feet dangling while they read or wrote in their journals. A young man was perched on a bench under the eaves of the roof that surrounded the courtyard area. He was playing lazily on a guitar. On the opposite side of the courtyard a short, burly man with intense dark eyes, black hair and beard, looked up at me as he chipped away at a large totem he was carving. It was supported horizontally by several boards lying crosswise under the eaves and took up most of the available seating space to the left of the fountain.

The main entrance opens into a large room that serves as kitchen and central gathering place. It was nicely furnished with a long wooden table and some smaller tables along the walls. Several wooden benches and chairs provided additional seating and there was plenty of counter space for food preparation. New appliances—stove, oven and refrigerator were lined-up against the far wall near a large sink. A variety of pots and pans and cooking utensils were in evidence.

The overseer of the complex stood to greet me as I stepped into the room. He shook my hand and welcomed me as if I'd just arrived at his home. When I'd signed the register and paid the fee, which was comparable to all other less appealing *refugios*, he showed me to my room. Several sleeping rooms opened off of the two hallways on either side of the kitchen. They were broken into sizes to fit only six or eight very comfortable beds. There was also a room for a family traveling together to share. The up-to-date bathrooms were large enough for the groups of people that always gather at the washbasins and mirrors and, more importantly, they were very clean with plenty of hot water.

After I was given my room assignment, I followed my usual afternoon routine of showering and washing my laundry, changing into clean clothes and going out to look for someplace to hang the wet ones to dry.

Within the walled area, which kept the view of the city at bay, aside from the covered seating under the eaves, there were ample rows of rope for drying laundry toward the back of the grounds.

"Hey! Hi, Maureen!" I heard coming from behind me as I reached to hang my dripping clothes.

I turned to see Jan, the young American woman I'd met in León who had been sitting in the plaza with her friend as I arrived from the train station. *So—she did decide to walk!*

"Hi!" I said in return, "So you did it! Good for you!" She walked toward me across the pebbles that covered the ground beneath the flapping clothing. It was clear she was limping.

"Yeah, it's been fun and really interesting. I hurt my foot though—sprained it or something—so I'm staying here for a few days," she explained. "I have to clean and stuff but I don't mind. It's a great place. Did you meet the sculptor? Oh, you have to come and meet him and carve on his totem. Everybody's doing it!"

When I had finished hanging my clothes, Jan took me by the arm and shepherded me back to the courtyard to introduce me to Juan. He didn't speak English but he knew Jan was trying to make me feel "at home." I thought he might be Spanish but he never said a word—just gestured with his hands and his eyes. Boring into me with those intense dark eyes, he handed me a wood-carving tool, of which there were many lying on the bench where he was sitting. I shook my head and said, "No, no thanks, I don't want to." I don't know why I didn't want to carve on his phallic totem. I handed the tool back to him.

"Oh, everybody's done a little something. Come on, Maureen," Jan pleaded. "He's been given permission to stay here until he finishes the whole thing and then they're going to install it right here in the courtyard," she said with obvious excitement. I had an image of his phallic representation of his experience of the Camino memorialized in this peaceful setting. I told her I might do a little carving later on but that first I wanted to do some drawing and write in my journal while my feet soaked.

The Totem Carver seemed lecherous to me. Wasn't it obvious to Jan? He made no secret of his surveillance of each woman who passed within his range. As I stood in front of him, he seemed to look at every part of my body except my eyes. He was walking the Camino with a woman half his age—Jan later explained—someone he had met in France. Jan thought they weren't getting along very well though and, in fact, she thought maybe she had a chance with him. "Isn't he sexy?" she sighed.

I excused myself and walked away to explore the grounds before going for my journal. I followed the short path out to the small chapel I had seen when I entered the gate to the grounds. The exterior was very traditional looking. Probably early 12th century, Romanesque—simple, block-like—with very little ornamentation. The interior, however, had been completely decorated with contemporary paintings of the

Camino on the walls and ceiling. No religious images of saints or miracles—no crosses or crucifixes were depicted. And, later that day at the Pilgrims Blessing, there was no reference to God or any other religious figure. The first truly non-religious service I had found on the Camino.

The saint who the *refugio* was named after, Saint Nicolas de Flüe, was from the same village as the benefactor of the *refugio* and the only Swiss saint recognized by the Catholic Church. His was the only name and image you saw there. He lived from 1417 to 1487 and at the age of fifty, after marrying, having ten children, being involved in civic duties, he became a hermit. He spent his last twenty years praying and advising people who came to him. His beliefs were founded on brotherly love and universal peace. I wondered if that included the wife he left with the ten children.

The day was still warm but pleasant. I decided not to take my usual afternoon *siesta* and went to the room, retrieved my journal and carried it out to the foot-soaking fountain.

Only one man was reading a book there when I took up my place on the edge of the pool. I sat at the end farthest from the door into the building and closest to the gate leading into the compound from the street. A half an hour or so had passed. For a moment in time everyone sitting around the courtyard, under the eaves, or on the patio, hanging laundry or chatting seemed to be in a state of suspension. Everything was very quiet except for the tap, tap, tapping of Don Juan carving on his totem. I looked up from my journal and studied what looked to me to be a tableau or stage set. People walking near me appeared to move in slow motion. I became aware of women yelling and a child crying desperately, somewhere nearby. Looking around at the people sitting with me in the courtyard, I had the sense that they didn't hear the raucous shrieking and wailing. I shrugged my shoulders to the man sitting at the fountain with me with an expression of "What's that all about?" he just shrugged in return and went back to reading.

From my perch I turned to look all around me and finally located the two women who were the source of the yelling. They were standing outside the compound, framed by the opening in the wall where the gate was. *Who are these women?* I thought. *What are they doing here? There's no house around here, no store they might be going to or coming from.*

It sounded like their argument was escalating and there was going to be a violent fight at any minute. I started to feel anxious. The atmosphere was heavy with the anger and negativity of the two women and yet, looking around at the others, no one else in the compound seemed in the least disturbed by it. I swung my feet out of the pool and walked over to the gate. There, standing directly outside the gate on the sidewalk, almost centered in an image that looked somehow staged, I saw two heavy-set, young women in simple cotton dresses. They were a mere six inches from each other's faces, bent in aggressively towards each other—locked in masks of anger. One of the women seemed completely out of control and I wondered if she was going to hit the other woman. A little girl of about three- or four-years old stood next to the one who seemed deranged, crying and pleading, "Mamma, Mamma! No, Mamma, no!" as she tugged on the skirt of the crazed woman.

I was suddenly shaken with an overwhelming feeling that I didn't understand and can't yet explain. Everything became very, very still. No thoughts busied my mind and yet I had a profound sense of knowing. A long forgotten scene entered my mind in a flash—as if playing out on a screen. It was a lost memory that seemed to have been struggling to surface and now burst forth:

The actors on that would-be screen were very much like those I was watching outside the gate. The screaming voice was my mother's. I was the little girl standing very close to her, gripping the fabric of her soft cotton dress with one hand, rubbing my tear-swollen eyes with the other. I held my head down and could see my mother's shoes— barely visible through the fog of my tears. The other woman stood a few inches from her. My stomach started to hurt. My head felt dizzy.

The two women were raging at each other in a crescendo that catapulted me out of the path of their violent shoving and on to the ground nearby. There was a lot of confusion and I remember seeing other people running into the circle beginning to gather around my mother. The yelling had stopped. All I felt was terror. Is it possible that I recalled being carried to a place nearby? I can't be sure. My only remaining image of that day is seeing someone walk my mother away. She had silver bracelets on. Was it a dream? Did her demons and angry psyche so completely invade my mind that I created this memory to make sense of it? Whatever the truth of the events of that day so long ago, I stood there that afternoon in Ponferrada with a profound sense of peace about how it was my brother and I were sent to the orphanage. In my head I was screaming, *She didn't give me away!*

How singularly different the two explanations were. It was as though someone had ripped open the envelope that held the secret and it was being read to me. I now knew the answer to that life-long question—the question that Grace wouldn't answer. She was unable to tell me the truth about the incident that added to her self-loathing—her deep shameful secret. Every interaction my family had was layered with the remains of a sense of failure; a sense of a lost opportunity to ever get it "right." Even I took part in keeping the secret, though I never knew what it was. My participation came with my willingness to assume the embarrassment and the unnamed shame. We were all co-conspirators.

Some say the magic of the Camino is that it always teaches you something you didn't know you had to learn. It almost always teaches humility, patience, forbearance, and understanding. As you walk and meet other pilgrims, after a while it becomes obvious that each person is walking his or her own Camino. One person's experience of the walk is completely unlike another's—just as in life—simply because of what he's brought along. The Architect's need for a job, Diana from Quebec's physical pain and grief, Hanna's desire to be someone she's not, are all examples of the burdens they were carrying. I carried the burden of my mother long before I put the box of her ashes in my backpack and started to walk to Santiago. Given the things most of us are carrying with us, be they goals, or an injustice, or a misunderstanding, or a need, we're all doing the best we can in our efforts to reach our Santiago.

There were still questions in my mind. The one that loomed over me was, *Where was my father?* If he had been around, we wouldn't have been taken away. That must have been one of the times he had left her. But the details didn't seem to matter any more. I felt the truth of my "revelation," and realized the need for me to forgive my mother. She was walking her own path and doing the best she could with what she brought along with her.

I read somewhere that Grace is the spirit that exists in us for the sole purpose of giving us strength. One of the beliefs about the magic of the Camino is—you start out with a prayer (or an idea) and end with a miracle.

We don't receive wisdom;
we must discover it for ourselves
after a journey that no one can take for us
or spare us.

Marcel Proust

Walking Stick and Dancing Shoes were ahead of me a couple of days before, somewhere on the mountain path west of Astorga. I gave them their moniker because she used a long, carved, wooden walking stick, almost equal to her height, and he tied a pair of sandals to the outside of his backpack. With the movement of his walking, the shoes looked like they were dancing along behind him. I admired their steady pace and seemingly quiet nature even though for many days I had only seen them from behind. Later I learned that they had begun their walk straight out of their own front door in Marseilles, putting them well ahead of anyone else I met for walking the longest distance to Santiago—more than 1,000 miles.

They were ahead of me once again as I struggled to find a Camino marker leaving Ponferrada. Except for seeing them, I thought I was definitely lost a second time that morning. The first time I had gotten confused and not seen the markers when I left the refugio in the morning light. In fact, I was so mixed up at my first attempt— wondering if I was following the markers back out of town, going east, rather than through town, going west—that I decided to retrace my steps back to the refugio and start all over again. With one last leering stare, some pointing, hand gestures, and head nodding from Don Juan the Totem Carver, I was on the path toward Santiago again.

The temperature in the mountains was more bearable than it had been in the flat lands on the way out of Astorga. Sometime in the late morning I passed a grove of verdant trees, set well off the dusty path. The sweet smell of grasses and wildflowers in a nearby field created a magical aura about the scene. There was a stream with lush, yellow-green foliage bordering it and, in my imagination, I saw The Dutch Couple Who Picnic resting there, waving to me as I walked on. Ever encouraging as they were, I took the vision as a sign that I should relax my pace a bit and enjoy a leisurely lunch on the grass, as they would have.

A few miles further I came to the village of Cacabelos and looked for a grocery store to buy something a little different than my usual yogurt, fruit, and snack bar for lunch. Whatever I was going to eat, I was committed to taking it to a field or under a grove of trees further along on the path outside of town. Stepping down into a small *mercado* on a side street off the marked Camino, an attractive, rosy-cheeked woman stood behind the counter.

"Buenos dias, señora!" she sang out. *"Qué desea?"*

No other customers were in the store—I was the center of her attention. I quietly attempted the words, *"queso, por favor?"* with the hope of getting some cheese. The variety of local cheeses she had was amazing—and mouth-watering. She gave me small tastes of several. I chose a large piece of a soft goat cheese, the name of which I tried to pronounce (which amused the *señora*), an orange, some radishes, two tomatoes, a can of sardines, a large bottle of water and a whole loaf of fresh, crusty, unsliced bread. For dessert, a dozen small chocolate cookies dusted with powdered sugar and a half-liter container of milk. The woman bagged my lunch and took the large euro bill I handed her, slowly counting out the change into my outstretched hand with the utmost patience and a lovely smile.

"Muchas gracias, señora, gracias!" she said, *"Buen Camino, señora! Vaya con dios!"* All the while, her head bobbing and hand waving with a kind of reverence that made me wonder either she seldom had pilgrims visit her store or she was very impressed with all I planned to eat for lunch. Or maybe she was just another example of how people everywhere want to offer a smile, some kindness or encouragement, if we would only look for it. Because of the solitary, repetitive nature of the walk, the little kindnesses and simple exchanges I had with people were significant to me and held more meaning than I would ordinarily have given them.

Perched on a rock in the shade at the edge of a field, I ate while I studied the folded paper guide I'd picked-up at the *refugio* in León. It was a daily pastime to make calculations using the distances listed there. Where would I get food? Where would I sleep?

Ponferrada	13.5 miles to Villafranca
Cacabelos	how much further to Villafranca?
Villafranca del Bierzo (steep climb)	11.5 miles to Reutelan
Reutelan (most intense climb)	6.5 miles to O Cebreiro
O Cebreiro (18 m. from Villafranca)	13 + miles to Triacastela
Triacastela (stay at refugio?)	9+ miles to Sarria
Samos	
Sarria (18+ miles to Gurzon)	14.5 miles to Portomarin
Portomarin	4 miles to Gurzon
Gurzon	12 miles to Casanova
Casanova	14+ miles to Arzua
Palais de Rei	
Melide (breakfast here?)	
Arzua	20 miles to Monte de Gozo
Monte de Gozo	3 miles to Santiago
Santiago	

Just about 122 to 125 miles left to go. Wow! I could be in Santiago in six—maybe seven days . . . if all goes well.

It was on my way to Villafranca del Bierzo that day that I had the only two sexually threatening experiences I was to have on the entire Camino. Both were so similar—one, just as I was leaving Ponferrada, and the other as I was approaching Villafranca—that I thought maybe it was the "style" of the young men of the region. In both cases, the men sat in a car, which was pulled-up close to the Camino, facing an on-coming walker. When the walker was a single woman, he called out to her to have her approach the car and offered the woman a view of what his hand was doing in his lap. I shared my story with a Dutch woman who was also walking alone and she said she had the same thing happen to her when she walked from Ponferrada to Villafranca. These things have a way of catching on.

The most frightening of the two times was when I had lost the path markers on the way to Villafranca for the third time that day and was walking with no other pilgrims in sight for a couple of hours. I was a little feverish with the cold I was trying to ignore. A lone car sat facing me on a dirt road that ran through a field, adjacent to a vineyard. The area was desolate. Throughout the whole afternoon, only two or three cars had passed me on the paved road where I'd been walking. I finally spotted a small sign with an arrow that directed me to the *refugio* in Villafranca where I had planned to stay the night. It was pointing in the very direction where the car was parked.

The young, dark, mustached man sitting behind the wheel called out and gestured to me to come closer. This time I knew better than to be so agreeable and continued walking, picking up my pace and ultimately breaking into a run up the hill. I looked back to see that he had started his car and was turning around. I ran faster. My heart was pounding. Sweat was pouring down my face and into my eyes as I desperately dashed in between the rows of the planted vineyard. Blinded by my panic, I ran to the top row of the vineyard and dove into a bramble of bushes and through a cover of trees that edged the planted field. From there I could see through the undergrowth to a road that lead down a hill and into Villafranca. I arrived at the *refugio* panting and unable to speak.

The owners of the *refugio* in Villafranca are a friendly family and, even though the place itself is like a construction site—they had a fire a few years before and were still rebuilding—the accommodations were pleasant enough. The father was said to be a healer and when I had another episode of fever, shakes, and delirium, he "laid his hands" on me and pronounced me "cured." I did feel better but I'm not sure if it was his hands passing over my breasts and caressing my bottom that did it. Maybe it was the sleep I had or the aspirins his wife gave me. Another pilgrim there told me that my symptoms were classic signs of heat stroke. The diagnosis sounded reasonable.

That evening dinner was served in the main room, cooked by the woman who ran the place with her husband and sons. Several of us dined on five courses of a delicious tomato soup, broiled fish, potatoes and fresh greens from the garden, a mixed-green salad, and a pudding-like cake for dessert. There was plenty of dark rich red wine, bread, sparkling water, and seconds on dessert. It was a grand feast—everything wonderfully tasty and fresh. Certainly the best meal I had on the whole Camino and all for what was comparable to about seven U.S. dollars.

Walking Stick and Dancing Shoes, Michéle ("only one l ") and Bernard, were among those who shared the dinner at the broad wooden table that night. Both of them were practicing Catholics and Walking Stick, in particular, wanted to understand her religion better. She was thinking about it and questioning its meaning as she walked. Bernard had recently retired and had no dilemma that he was considering.

Walking Stick, Michéle, had lived with a family in Scotland during high school and spoke nearly perfect English. She was also fluent in Spanish, Italian, German—and, of course, her native French. If she ever felt burdened as interpreter, not only at dinner that night but also all along the Camino, she never shrunk from being helpful. She was very likeable and the only woman friend I sat and talked with for any length of time along the whole Camino—aside from Hanna, of course. But that was different.

"From Marseille to Santiago we will walk, step-by-step, 1,713 kilometers!"(1,065 miles) Michéle said excitedly. "I want to arrive there on my birthday, June 8th. We left on the 30th of March and, if we get there on the 8th of June, we will have been two months and ten days."

"Wow! That's the date I want to arrive, too!" I replied. "It's my son's birthday, too! What a coincidence, huh?"

Someone asked her when she first knew of the Camino and how she and Bernard had become so passionate about walking it.

"I learned of the Camino at school, in history. I was about eleven. Bernard was younger. It was at catechism. But at that time it meant nothing. Later I read *Therapy*, of David Lodge—you know this book? I found the experience lived by the heroine was so moving that I dreamed of living the same experience. I bought magazines, books of the Camino, books written by people who walked to Santiago. And I dreamed a lot. I first walked in my head," Michéle went on.

"On the Camino you always have the impression that everything has a deep meaning. We cry so much on the Camino, not sobbing, no, but our eyes are often running. Could you say that? 'Running' as when the nose is running? Also, you know, you always meet the right person at the right moment; it's the magic of Santiago. Like here—tonight!" she exclaimed as she lifted her wine glass in a toast to us all.

Michéle laughed when I told her the names I had given them. Her father had carved the walking stick in 1996 especially for the day when she would make her pilgrimage to Santiago. He died in 2001 before they set out on their Camino, so she felt particularly identified with the stick and thought it fitting that I referred to her that way. Before she left Marseilles it was three inches longer.

Traversing the valley of the *Rio Bierzo* and ascending into the mountainous region west of the river took all of the next damp, cool day. The climb was wet in the morning with foggy drizzle and gray skies all day. At Ruetelan I decided to stop for the day and find a place to get warm and dry. There was a room available in a private house that had a sign for pilgrims. There were only a few rooms—most were private—for one or two people. The hostel was run by a dark and burly middle-aged man who played the guitar in the evening and woke everyone the next morning with Beethoven's 9th Symphony, the "Ode to Joy," blasting from his CD player. He cooked a delicious breakfast of eggs and potatoes and sausage and toasted muffins with plenty of coffee. Before leaving, you were asked to stop into his "office" where he tallied your bill and wished you *"Buen Camino."*

The walk between Ruetelan and O'Cebreiro was another day of climbing, climbing, climbing. The skies had cleared and displayed an intense blue. Except for navigating the rain-soaked muddy path, the clear air at those elevations made for a comfortable walk. My strength was evident.

After the startling realization I had in Ponferrada about my brother and I being taken away from Grace, the conflicting ideas of keeping a family secret that I didn't even know, had left me. No longer did I harbor the sense of shame about Grace's mental disorders, or her neglect and abuse. The unconscious loyalty that plagued me all my life had finally lifted. It was miraculous to have had the child's sense of "What did I do wrong?" disappear into nothing. Knowing the truth about the events that happened that catapulted my family and me into a sense of shame had truly allowed me to "move on" not only physically, but emotionally as well. My backpack was not only lighter, but my whole being soared with the freedom that came when I finally just let go of the burden— the belief that held no good purpose. There were days when I could hardly believe how many miles I had walked with little or no effort. Could the calculations I made on the torn and wrinkled guide be right? I had actually found the wings The Irish Priest assured me of.

When I reached the higher elevations on the path that day, where the trail seemed to cling to the side of the mountain, the astonishing vistas of the green mountains and valleys in the distance were awe-inspiring. Far below were snaking lines worn into the rocky earth by foraging goats and heavy-burdened mules that carried goods through those mountains for centuries. A pilgrim above and ahead of me on the path called out to a muleteer who stood with his packed mule way below us. His *"buenos dias,"* echoed across the entire valley.

On the rounded clearing at the summit of *Monte O'Cebreiro*, the isolated village of the same name sits where a miracle took place. The small settlement is comprised of round, thatch-roofed houses with the air of a fairy tale town where trolls live. In the 14th century a miracle happened there which involved a peasant from a nearby village. A devout man climbed through a snowstorm to attend Mass at the small stone church of St. Mary. He arrived just as the priest was blessing the bread and wine. When the priest questioned the peasant's motives in coming to the church through such a blizzard (not trusting the man's devotion) the bread and the wine were transformed into flesh and blood.

After lighting a candle for Grace in the little church, I walked around the charming settlement and then found the path on to Santiago.

Galicia, the green, western-most province in Spain, looked and felt like Vermont where I'd lived years before. The green rolling hills and meadows gave me the warm sense of arriving at last at someplace familiar. The farms and small villages that the path crossed through though were some of the poorest I'd ever seen.

That day was spent tramping through muddy, manure-packed roads right next to houses that looked no more substantial than the shelters cobbled together for the farmer's cows and work horses. The sound of chained and penned barking dogs and the pervasive smell of manure stayed with me for the entire first day in Galicia.

Most farms throughout the province have an interesting structure that's particular to the region. Much like corncribs you see on old farms in the States, these granaries or *horreos* were used to store corn also, as well as other grains. The *horreos* come in all styles but they all look like small houses and they stand a couple of feet above ground on legs, often with a tile-covered, gabled roof and open-worked sides. They're no longer practical for farmers today but they remain on properties and, in fact, some people have them built just to add charm to more contemporary buildings.

Not long after descending from O'Cebreiro, the path passes the short stone obelisk that marks 100 kilometers distance to Santiago. Covered in graffiti and laden with mementos left by pilgrims, the marker is the beginning of the Camino for some weekend walkers and short-term pilgrims. The full blessings are said to be available to anyone who walks at least the last 100 kilometers (about 62 miles) and so there's an obvious increase in traffic from that point on. With the swelling numbers of people walking, there was more litter, more noise, and more crowded *refugios*.

The *refugios* themselves throughout Galicia are standardized contemporary buildings mostly uniform in materials, number of beds, and size. Someone locally is delegated overseer and each is managed very loosely. Arriving at one, no manager showed-up to open the building until late in the day. He was in his fields and would come when he was finished planting, a sign read. At another, no one ever showed-up but thankfully, the building was open. Still another was so remotely located that there was nowhere for miles around to buy food. If you arrived at the *refugio* with nothing in your pack, you just didn't eat that night. The next morning there would be a long walk to get a cup of coffee.

It may be that the satisfaction need
depends on my going away,
so that when I've gone and come back,
I'll find it at home.

Rumi

Santiago, June 8th

Hola, dear ones,

I walked into Santiago this morning as the sun was
rising—tears streaming down my face. I made it!

As I walked through the gate that led down a narrow
road to the plaza in front of the Cathedral, there was a
bedraggled young man standing playing a Celtic tune
on his violin. His thin, shorthaired hound dog stood at
attention next to him and beside a basket meant for
donations. I was the only person the troubadour was
serenading and, just as with the cowbells that heralded
the beginning of my walk at Roncesvalles, I took his
melody as a proclamation of my triumphant completion.
Karen Z. had warned me that tourists often line-up in the
plaza to take photos of "real" pilgrims. Celebrity status!

Last night I slept at *Monte do Gozo* where the pilgrims traditionally washed themselves in the river before entering Santiago. Alas, now there are hundreds of showers at a huge hostel that's like a city in itself: laundromat, a big cafeteria, restaurant, etc. Large crowds of young people partied all night. The police came to break up a brawl. Thankfully, my earplugs were handy.

The last 20 miles yesterday were difficult. I was tired— tired of all the noisy people on the path. Where had all the quiet gone? The highlight of the afternoon came when three bikes flew past me and then all came to a stop a few feet ahead. "It's you!" the lead biker chimed. It was The Mexican Boy Scouts, still in uniform! Marco told me they had been biking since Burgos. I mentioned that I had seen them on their bikes there. We hugged— it was such a happy time. They heard I had to stop in Santo Domingo and started again but didn't know whether or not I got to the *Cruz de Ferro*. Marco walked with me awhile, as he had before. No pain this time. Feet, fine. Knees, fine.

Later, at a marker just outside of Santiago, The Savior was parked along the side of the road, handing out water to any takers. I stopped to talk with him as I had on the *Sierra del Perdón*, weeks before. He was genuinely pleased that I had made it and said he had been asking about me all along the Camino. A journalist and a photographer from a Spanish magazine cut our conversation short. They wanted to interview both The Savior and The Boy Scouts. I declined to take part and walked on.

The Scouts were at the office later where you receive your "Compostela." A document that certifies your completion of the Camino. Your name and country

are recorded and how much distance you covered on foot (it must be at least 100 kilometers). Later, at the Pilgrim's Mass in the Cathedral, you're included in the numbers of those who completed the Camino that week. The service is very moving. I stood in tears, looking around at the grandeur of it all. It was a very emotional time. Seeing faces in the crowd that had become familiar to me was such a joy.

There were The Gruppo Spañiardos, still talking while the service was taking place; the four sisters who would set an alarm clock to wake themselves (and everyone else) for the last couple of mornings; The Mexican Boy Scouts, Diana from Quebec, who walked in with no evidence of braces but still carried so much sadness; the young Silent Nun who was my only witness at Grace's service at the *Cruz de Ferro*; The Brazilian Brigade—without their fearless leader—but Romeo had his arm around a lady (ah, success); two middle-aged Norwegian women who walked in halter tops and shorts, looking for romance and arrived looking like lobsters. (One struck up a romance with a Frenchman—too bad, she couldn't speak French but "loved him deeply," nevertheless.)

Walking Stick and Dancing Shoes were across the aisle from where I stood during the service. It made me sad to learn that Michéle had a sense of loss about her faith. She explained that it was as if she had walked all along the Camino with a treasure, in a coffer, and the day she arrived in Santiago, she opened it and found it was empty. I hope her depression was due to exhaustion and nothing more long lasting. I'll probably never see any of these wonderful people again.

There were others that I hadn't seen in weeks. So many familiar faces of people I had walked with, ate a meal

with, met at a *refugio,* or passed on the trail—everyone
there celebrating life in his or her own way in the
beauty of that magnificent building.

It's hard to imagine how pilgrims hundreds of years
ago felt walking into the Cathedral after having finally
made it to Santiago! The gold-covered altars, carvings,
sculptures, candles; the soaring heights of the space, and
the colors reflected from the stained glass windows—
all contributing to the awe-inspiring beauty. A huge
incense burner, the *botafumeiro,* hangs on heavy chains
from somewhere on high. At noon every day it's swung
in a wide arc during the Pilgrim's Mass, giving a
memorable scent to the service. Inside the massive
west doorway at the *Portico de la Gloria,* pilgrims touch
a certain column to signify the end of their pilgrimage.
Most walk below the altar through a narrow stairway
to see the case where St. James' bones are kept.
I did it all.

After the service, The Cologne Chorale and I had lunch
and drinks at an outdoor cafe on the main street running down from the Cathedral. We saw several others
we had met along the path who approached our table
and sat for awhile. There were tears of joy at our
reunions, hugs, congratulations. Some simply nodded,
waved, smiled, and walked on and with those gestures,
there was much said.

This has been a profound experience. There's never
been a time in my life when I've been so completely
focused on one step at a time. The first part, in carrying
Grace's ashes, was very hard but, as when you put
down any burden at long last, I was made stronger
because of it. Lost in my thoughts for days, I found clarity
and a far greater understanding of many so-called
obstacles that just aren't there. I met wonderful people

and when I did walk into the Cathedral with them, I was walking in to "thank God for my beautiful life."

Later today I'll search out the main post office and pick up the package of unnecessary things that I mailed to myself from Santo Domingo. I'm staying here at the large former dormitory of a monastery where most pilgrims rest at the end of their walk, then I'll take a bus to Finisterra (the end of the earth) for a few days at the beach there. Back to Madrid on Saturday for a day to see the Prado and then—HOME.

Since I've learned that _all_ of life is a Camino—even the rainy days, even the sad days, even the scary days— I send you the greeting all pilgrims give each other, _"Buen Camino!"_ Enjoy the walk!

Much love to you all,

Maureen

SUGGESTED READING

My entire experience on the Camino might have been very much enriched had I taken advantage of any of the wonderful books that are available in preparing oneself for the walk. Here are some I've read since returning:

Cousineau, Phil (1998), *The Art of Pilgrimage*, Conari Press, Berkeley.

Hitt, Jack (1994), *Off the Road: A Modern-Day Walk Down the Pilgrim's Route into Spain*, Simon and Schuster, New York.

Lack, Katherine (2003), *The Cockleshell Pilgrim, A Medieval Journey to Compostela*, SPCK, London.

Nooteboom, Cees (1997) translation by Ina Rilke, *Roads to Santiago: A Modern-Day Pilgrimage Through Spain*, Harcourt, San Diego.

Sumption, Jonathan (2003), *The Age of Pilgrimage: The Medieval Journey to God*, Hidden Spring Press, Mahwah.

The one book I did read before I left and enjoyed for its thorough coverage of the history of the Camino:

Aviva, Elyn (2001), *Following the Milky Way: A Pilgrimage on the Camino de Santiago*, 2nd ed., Pilgrims' Process, Boulder.

The ersatz guidebook, which was lost along the way was comprised of pho-tocopied pages from the Lonely Planet Publication, *Walking in Spain*, 2nd ed. (1999).

The Confraternity of Saint James, headquartered in London, publishes many English language guides to the Camino that are very practical and regularly updated. *Pilgrim Guides to Spain, 1. The Camino Francés*, has an almost step-by-step description of the path from Saint-Jean-Pied-de-Port in France to Santiago de Compostela. (www.csj.org.uk)

I first read about the Camino in an article written by Abigail Seymour, *"Ultreya!"* printed in a 1998, US Airways in-flight magazine, *Attaché*, page 58. Abigail has now walked the Camino two times and is presently living in North Carolina, working as a photographer, a mother, and still writing. Her beautiful photographs can be seen on her website: www.abigailseymour.com

Made in the USA
Charleston, SC
19 March 2013